A NATION UNDER GOD

Other books by David Holloway:
The Church and Homosexuality (ed.)
Where Did Jesus Go?
The Church of England—where is it going?

A Nation under God

DAVID HOLLOWAY

KINGSWAY PUBLICATIONS
EASTBOURNE

ISBN 0 86065 479 6

Front cover design by Vic Mitchell

Printed in Great Britain for
KINGSWAY PUBLICATIONS LTD
Lottbridge Drove, Eastbourne, E. Sussex BN23 6NT by
Richard Clay Ltd, Bungay, Suffolk.
Typeset by CST, Eastbourne.

Contents

Introduction

The Greek philosopher Aristotle somewhere says that you
should not write a book on politics or ethics until you are
fifty! I haven't yet reached that magic age, but I have just
recently retired from the Board for Social Responsibility of
the General Synod of the Church of England, on which I
served for ten years. So I can consider myself in retirement
from this commitment at least, if not from many others!

In writing this book I have four aims. First, I simply want
to put down on paper certain convictions I have about
'public life' that do not necessarily come onto the agenda of
church Boards for Social Responsibility. These relate to
fundamental questions about our national culture and the
place of the church in that culture. How, for example, do
society, politics and Christianity relate? What does it mean
for the church to get 'involved'? And, above all, how are
Christian people to see their responsibilities in the nation at
the end of the twentieth century? I shall not be referring to

specific issues of political debate, but rather to the underlying issues that so often get forgotten.

Secondly, I want to encourage Christians to allow their
faith to be properly established in the 'Public Square' in
Britain. For too long the church has accepted 'client status'.
And it appears to be apologizing for turning up to the party!
This should stop. Of course, all forms of triumphalism must
be avoided, but in a nation whose public faith is symbolized
by the Queen as 'the Supreme Governor of the Church of
England' and is therefore a nation with a Christian ethos,
there should be greater confidence. My experience is that
there is always interest when the church (thoughtfully)
points to Jesus Christ as the Way, the Truth and the Life for
society as well as for individuals. This is not least because of
the present lack of spiritual direction in the nation at large.

Thirdly, I want to say something 'strong' about broadcasting in Britain. No study of contemporary society is complete without reflection on the influence on the culture of
television and radio. So Christians need to think about
broadcasting. The Peacock Report on financing the BBC is
probably more significant than has been realized. That is
because broadcasting itself is more significant than most
people realize. And the Report dealt with more than
finance. For too long we have simply accepted with almost
august reverence the broadcasting establishment. Peacock is
asking questions about whether that is right.

Fourthly, I have a more ambitious aim. It is to get Christian questions into the discussion at the time of Parliamentary and local elections. It is not a matter of indifference
what our MPs or local councillors believe, what values they
have, or for that matter how they behave. It is worth know-
ing, too, how they vote. We should be far more issue orientated in Britain and far less party orientated. The Sunday
trading issue in 1986 showed what a coalition of Christians

and other people could achieve. Why shouldn't committed Christians continue to exercise a level of leadership not in a partisan way, but where the issues demand it?

David Holloway
Newcastle-upon-Tyne
August 1986

I

April Fools

It would be unfair to describe the chief actors in the month of April 1986 as April fools, but that April was no ordinary month and many thought some very foolish things were being done. Huge question marks appeared over public affairs in the United Kingdom, Europe, the United States and the USSR. It was not just that political judgements were questioned. Rather it was that some basic assumptions of government and social development were being challenged in a new way.

For a start, there were many people asking quite fundamental questions about international and domestic rights and wrongs. It was evident that not only the East but also the West was lacking an agreed morality. Yet, paradoxically, at the same time there were signs of a recovery of moral thinking. All this was making some very tricky political problems even more problematic. Add to all that two sobering and tragic reminders that twentieth century man was as fallible, and thus as human, as ever, and you had a very significant month. What had been going on?

International events

On Tuesday, April 15th at 2 am (local time), American F111 jet bombers, having taken off from bases in Britain, attacked Tripoli and Benghazi in Libya. Later on that same day the United States Presidential spokesman, Mr Larry Speakes, briefed the press: 'US forces have executed a series of carefully planned air strikes against terrorist targets,' he said.[1] It was estimated that 100 people had been killed, including the baby daughter of the Libyan leader, Colonel Muammar Gadaffi. More were injured, including his two young sons. There was immediately fierce debate in Britain, Europe and around the world about the United States' action and Mrs Thatcher's collaboration with the Americans.

But what was conspicuous about this heated debate in the British Parliament and media was that morality hardly entered into the discussion. It was all about self-interest. The main criterion for judging the rightness or wrongness of the action was whether the British, at home or abroad, would be more or less likely to be the objects of Arab terrorist attacks themselves. None of the old-fashioned moral criteria of the just war seemed to come into the reckoning. Once upon a time people would have asked about such an action: 'Is the action legally authorized? Is the cause a just one? Is the motive right? Is there discrimination (for you mustn't just kill indiscriminately)? And is the action proportionate to the alleged offence?' Some took this as a sign of serious moral bankruptcy.

But thirteen days later, as the month was drawing to a close, an event happened that quite eclipsed the Libyan affair. At 9 am on Monday, April 28th, technicians in Sweden's Forsmark nuclear power plant saw disturbing bleeps on their computer screens. The bleeps represented high levels of radiation and spelt danger with a capital 'D'. The workers at the plant were then tested and their clothing was found to be giving off very high radiation levels. They had no idea why. Their plant was in good order. But then twelve hours later at 9 pm on Moscow Television came a four-sentence statement from the Council of Ministers:

> An accident has taken place at the Chernobyl power station, and one of the reactors was damaged. Measures are being taken to eliminate the consequences of the accident. Those affected by it are being given assistance. A government commission has been set up.[2]

And that was all—for the moment. The brevity was taken as a cover-up; and a panic of ignorance swept over otherwise sober people. The whole story is now known and history. The people in that area, eighty miles to the north of Kiev, will find it hard to forget the nightmare of April 1986 for a long time to come. But the significance of Chernobyl was more than that of being the worst ever peace-time nuclear disaster.

Human failure

Its significance was underlined by another tragedy that came to the full light of day that April of 1986—the American *Challenger* disaster. The previous January the space craft had been launched. A puff of smoke less than half a second after its solid rocket boosters were ignited showed that something was seriously wrong. In fact there was going to be a fearful disaster, and millions saw it throughout the world in gruesome action replay on television. They saw the external fuel tank explode nine miles up, disintegrating the orbiter and killing all the crew.

But then came the inquiry. President Reagan set up a commission that reported in April. And what were their findings? *The Times* described them as indicating that the whole preparation and launch was 'a remarkable story of poor management, safety sacrificed to cost-cutting and danger signs ignored or rationalized'.[3] In the United States, on prime-time television, people were seeing and hearing the 'boffins' of NASA being interrogated. They were shocked by what they saw and heard.

So what was the significance of the Chernobyl and *Challenger* disasters? It was in the negative reaction both disasters generated towards super-power technology. Here were scientists and engineers supposed to be among the best the civilized world had ever produced. And what did you get? Failure, breakdown, incompetence and an inability to take quick remedial action.

So not only was there this feeling of moral bankruptcy in the developed world, as witnessed by the Libyan incident, but now a feeling of technical powerlessness. The major prop of twentieth century man—science—was being called into question. Of course, it was unfair; of course, nuclear power is a remarkable achievement; of course, the American space programme has much to be proud of. But certain events come together at certain times that change the psychology of a culture. If these disasters didn't quite do that, they at least opened a considerable chink in the armour! They proved that while 'man come of age' was brilliantly inventive, he was fallible; and they proved that he could never by his own efforts totally or ultimately transcend the primeval forces of nature or the inexorable facts of time, decay and death. That sort of 'salvation' has to come some other way. It has to come through religion.

So you would expect such a salvation to be discussed at the Council of the British Evangelical Alliance. However, as I was driving back from a Council meeting to Westminster at about this time with a fellow Council member, a Tory MP, the conversation was not so much about 'religion' as the chances of the Tory Government at the next General Election. But the two were not unconnected. 'If you have any

14

influence with the Prime Minister,' I suggested, 'try to get the message across that if the Tory Government succeeds in forcing the Shops Bill [commonly known as the Sunday Trading Bill] through the Commons, I can guarantee their failure at the next election. They will alienate the growing and significant Christian vote. It'll be the same as when the Liberals lost a lot of Christian support after the David Steel Abortion Bill.'

The number one story

It was Sunday Trading and all that went with it—the background campaign of opposition, the policy and tactics of the Government, and the result—that is to be seen as the number one story of April 1986. It was a portent of future developments and a symptom of late twentieth century Britain.

The opposition was an interesting coalition set up to defeat the Government, who wanted to deregulate shop opening hours. In it were some major retailing organizations as well as many small retailers; there was the shopworkers' union, USDAW; and there were the churches.

The issue, as with any issue of this sort, was complex. But more was at stake than met the eye. It was not just a question of 'sabbatarianism'. There was also the Government wanting to ride roughshod over the consciences of Christian Conservative MPs by imposing a whip to pass the proposed legislation.

Of course, the Sunday Trading laws in the country were in a mess and being abused. But it was always perfectly possible, given good will, to introduce alternative legislation. Some had made positive suggestions. So why deregulate? Answer: the big out-of-town super stores and garden and do-it-yourself centres were pushing for it. Many other traders did not want it. But, of course, once one started, all would have to follow if they were not to lose business. As the John Lewis Partnership (a major group opposed to the legislation) pointed out, at a football stadium the first person who stands up gets a better view, but soon everyone is standing instead of sitting and no one gets a better view!

Also, initially deregulation would be a face-saving exercise for the Government in terms of new jobs. But those would not have been full-time jobs, only part-time. Employment would fall in the long term, according to the Institute of Fiscal Studies. In the short term 500 full-time jobs would be lost, and in the long term 20,000.

But for the Christians opposed to the Bill the economic reasons were secondary. For them most important were the religious reasons. They spoke about the 'sabbath principle' as a 'creation ordinance'. That is to say, it comes in the Genesis narrative in the Bible *before* the account of man's Fall. Like marriage, it has to do with *man as such* and with the human condition generally. It has to do with the way we are made or created. So it was asserted that unless we have a one in seven days break we crack up. Indeed, the French Revolutionaries found that one in ten didn't work!

But what was wrong, it was asked, if each *individual* has one day off in seven? After all, many have to have 'individual' days off and work on Sundays—including clergymen! The answer was that the 'sabbath principle' of the seventh day means that the majority are to rest *at the same time*. This is because society as a whole, or a whole culture, needs a rest or a change of rhythm. The Christians added that true 're-creation' comes through the opportunity for worship as well as for rest and relaxation.

The Prime Minister's and opposition leaders' views

There were wide issues thrown up by this debate. These included fundamental questions of value. First, should quick-term economic profit always be put before the values of family life? The unions were arguing that the legislation would put a strain on married women, who would be forced to work on Sundays and neglect their families. Secondly, should the Government never weigh moral or religious considerations *on their own merits,* not just as a sop to voters? And, thirdly, should the Government ever seek to ride roughshod over the consciences of its supporters?

The public was interested in these issues, or a significant proportion of the public. Sensing this, the Jubilee Centre, a Christian study centre in Cambridge, got into action. It initiated the *Keep Sunday Special* campaign. It harnessed the support of the retailers and law enforcement officers as well as the churches. In 1985 Christopher Townsend and Michael Schluter wrote the well-argued Jubilee Centre Paper No 5, *Why Keep Sunday Special?* In April 1986, just before the key debate in Parliament, the campaign reached its climax. On Thursday, April 10th, the Archbishop of Canterbury Robert Runcie, Cardinal Basil Hume and the Moderator of the Free Church Federal Council Donald English, presented the Home Office with a petition, signed by over one million, to keep Sunday special. Yet even so, four days later, on the morning of the debate, the Government was still expecting a narrow win for their Sunday Trading Bill.

Earlier the General Synod of the Church of England had expressed its concern and opposition to the bill. This was reported to Government and Opposition leaders. The Synod received replies from the Prime Minister and leaders of opposition parties.[4] They were interesting.

Mrs Thatcher said she understood the Synod's concern 'to preserve the special nature of Sunday' but felt it was 'misplaced'. She did not want the character of Sunday to be altered, but the proposed bill would 'be of benefit to the many people who find present trading patterns inconvenient, without detriment to the character of Sunday'. She referred to the increasing number of married women in the workforce and the increase in home ownership. This was part of a changing pattern which added to the demand for longer shopping hours. She believed the findings of a survey that suggested that 'fewer than 30 per cent of shops will open regularly throughout the year on Sundays'.

Neil Kinnock, the leader of the Labour Party, said that while not personally opposed to Sunday Trading, he recognized strong arguments against it because of its effects on the traditional Sunday and on working conditions. He wanted 'rationalization of the anomalies', but any changes to the law should also include 'satisfactory protection for those whose working patterns would be changed'.

David Owen, the leader of the Social Democrats, said the proposed bill would 'profoundly change the way people treat Sunday'. He was prepared for changes to current legislation, but added, 'I do not believe that Sunday should be treated for trading purposes in exactly the same way as all the other days of the week.' He went on to say that 'market freedom is not desirable in all aspects of life . . . we have to balance market needs and social priorities'.

Government defeat

In the event the Government suffered a stunning defeat in the Commons over Sunday Trading. It was the first time that the Conservative Government had lost a bill on a second reading, the first such defeat for nine years, and the biggest revolt of Parliament under Mrs Thatcher. Sixty-eight Conservative backbenchers defied the three-line whip and voted against the Government. The House rejected the Bill by 296 votes to 282, a majority of 14.

In the debate Francis Pym said the Bill would impoverish people's lives, change the character of Sunday and have an effect the nation would live to regret. Sir Adam Butler said he was a practising member of the Church of England and a churchwarden. Parliament must not prejudice the need of everyone to have a break from routine. He, therefore, had no alternative but to oppose the principle of the Bill. Sir Bernard Braine said the Bill would lead to full-scale business activity on Sundays. It was about market shares and not a call for freedom. It was about destroying Sunday as a day set apart for the family.

Add to those rebel speeches an impassioned plea from Mr Donald Stewart, the leader of the Scottish National Party. He said that the Government could have no pretence after this Bill about belief in Christian morality. The Bill went directly against God's plan for living. The fourth Commandment was an integral part of the Law of God: the Sabbath Day should be kept holy!

And Mr Gerald Kaufman, the chief Opposition spokesman on Home Affairs, spoke powerfully as a Jew about the 'sabbath principle'. He admitted that, of course, for him the sabbath was Saturday, not Sunday. But the principle was the same.

My father [he said] was a Jewish immigrant to this country from Poland, a factory worker all his life. He never earned very much of a wage. He had a large and growing family to house, clothe and feed. But whatever it meant to his employment and promotion prospects he would never accept a job which required him to work on his Sabbath. For him, in his hard-working and often toilsome life, the Sabbath was held precious, a tranquil island in the stormy sea of the week. That is how many millions of people in this country feel about Sunday.

So the Government was defeated. Something truly significant had occurred. But unfortunately the nation had no time to digest and reflect on what it was. The reason was very simple. At the same time as the debate was going on in the House of Commons at Westminster, American F111 jets were flying down the east Atlantic on their way to Libya; and about the same time as MPs were voting, in the early hours of Tuesday morning, April 15th, the aircraft were bombing Libya. Inevitably the number one item on the radio and television news and in the press that Tuesday morning was the bombing. The debate in Parliament had to take second place. There was little time or space for analysis and comment on it. Such spare time or space as there was went to the uproar over the Libyan action.

A cloud no bigger than a man's hand

We must not exaggerate the significance of the defeat over Sunday Trading. But it would be foolish to ignore what this indicated. True, at present it may be no bigger than 'a cloud the size of a man's hand'. But it could indicate a significant amount of rain in the future! What, then, did this incident show? Two things.

First, it showed the political influence and sophistication of the 'new evangelicalism'. The Jubilee Centre is an evangelical Christian organization. Of course, in this campaign they co-ordinated many who were by no means card-carrying Christians, let alone evangelicals. But that is not the point. In any political activity there will be alliances. The point rather is that the members of the Jubilee Centre had the skill, expertise and motivation to *lead*. And that is always the crucial component—leadership. Here were people who foresaw a problem, analysed it well and took action, harnessing all sorts of interests—and they succeeded. Without their leadership the Government would not have been defeated. But it was defeated, well and truly.

This influence of the evangelicals, in time, is bound to grow. It is the political expression of the evangelical revival that has been going on in universities and colleges since the late fifties. Over the last two decades the largest single student bodies have not been the political societies, cultural societies or any other societies. They have been the Christian unions. These are groups of orthodox Christians, members of various denominations, who are all committed to a biblical and evangelical faith. They do not see Christianity fundamentally as an alternative political party, as do some Christian groups. They are not supportive of 'the social gospel'. They see man's need first of all as 'getting right with God'.

So, as students, they probably spend more time in straight evangelism than in political activism. But that is not to say that they do not have social concerns as secondary concerns. Nor is it to say that they expect their commitment to be private. The older they get (and many of them are now in positions of leadership in society and the professions), the more they believe very strongly that while Christianity should not necessarily be political in a party sense, it *should* be public. And while they do not expect (or want) all their values to be enforced by law, that is not to say that they believe their values should never *influence* the law.

Inevitably, with a growing self-confidence, they will be making their voices heard more frequently in public affairs; they will also be a growing factor for political parties to take note of when it comes to policies and manifestos—crudely, to vote-catching. Interestingly, evangelicals are already in key positions in political life. Not only are they in the opposition parties and opposing the Government. They have also been at the heart of Mrs Thatcher's own Government. They are on opposing political sides to each other, but that doesn't mean to say that on some clear issues they cannot work together, or at least in sympathy.

So, the first thing the defeat of the Government over Sunday Trading showed was the strength of the new evangelicalism; secondly it showed that the United Kingdom is by no means as secular as it is sometimes made out to be. Underneath is a considerable gut feeling of sympathy for religious values and beliefs, if not agreement. This is not reflected in church-going, where the current figures are very low. But surveys indicate, as we shall see, that a majority of the population of the United Kingdom likes to think of itself as Christian.

Edwin Robertson, the veteran religious broadcaster, makes interesting observations about the contemporary Sunday. He argues that there is almost a superstitious belief that it is good for society as a whole if churches are open and the devout are there in them praying for the rest. This is 'the divine in national life, and valued in a vague sort of way by that majority of non church-goers who tell the pollsters they still believe in God'.[5]

The received opinion that 'secularism rules OK' is wrong. That is why legislation that is perceived to be un-Christian or anti-Christian is on a very bad wicket.

2

A Crisis of Values

Is there really moral bankruptcy in Britain? Do we need a greater input from the Christian faith into public life? What is the real condition of the nation like as we move towards the end of the twentieth century?

A Gallup survey

In 1985 TV South produced a network television series entitled *Twenty Years On*. In it David Frost was trying to find out what Britain was like in the eighties by comparing it with Britain in the sixties. A specially commissioned Gallup poll was at the centre of the series. It focused on the underlying attitudes of people all over the country twenty years ago and in the present. The findings included these.

In the sixties only one marriage in sixteen ended in divorce; in the eighties it is one in three, the highest divorce rate in Europe (the figures on second and third marriages are even worse).

There are over one million single parent families. As David Frost said, 'Around seven million people in Britain today are step-fathers, step-daughters, step-somethings.' A social scientist commented to TVS, 'By the year 2,000 it's not going to be a question of how many children parents have, but of how many parents children have!'

Twenty years ago 37% of wives had jobs. Today it is 58%. However, both men and women feel, by a large majority (three out of four), that the children of working wives suffer in some way as a result.

In terms of the wider community, half of British men and women now believe that the country is a violent place in which to live. Happily, eight out of ten are still proud to be British. Probably one of the most frequently asked questions is: 'What is this country coming to?'

> 20 years ago [said David Frost], top of the list of groups we blamed for Britain's ills was the Government (35 per cent) (then Labour). And it's the same in 1985; we blame the Government —but even more so (46 per cent). And the people we blame next are the unions. In 1965 it was 1 in 5 and in 1985 it's gone up to 1 in 3.

Gallup also asked who were felt to be the least trustworthy group of people in Britain. The answer was MPs. They were closely followed by estate agents!

Two out of three people in Britain do not want to see any *single* party in power when the year 2,000 comes around. The majority want some form of coalition or national government.

The survey revealed that 'the rich vein of nostalgia about the sixties is linked with a feeling that the decade did not really deliver on its campaign manifesto'. In fact it ended up in 'disillusionment'—'The disillusionment of a whole society who found that "doing your own thing" on a hefty mortgage was not as easy as it sounded.' David Frost concluded:

> For the time being, we are better off, better informed and more efficient in our use of time. Our homes are brighter, we have

more amenities and we are more hedonistic. We also have less peace of mind, we are more frightened and more insecure. The country itself feels more ill-tempered, self-centred, more 'looking after No.1'.[1]

Where are we going?

Something is adrift. But the real problem is not so much the failure to answer the question, 'What is this country coming to?' but rather the failure to answer the question, 'Where is this country going?' It is national direction that we lack. There is no agreed destination, let alone destiny.

But *this* has been the underlying problem for the last twenty years (and more). In the 1966 General Election Edward Heath was leading the Conservatives in an unsuccessful attempt to unseat Harold Wilson's Labour Government. *The Times* on that occasion had this comment in its editorial: 'The election campaign is a tawdry business . . . The time is overdue for some political leader to take it by the scruff of the neck and lift it on to a plane worthy of its argument. What is at stake is the future of Britain.' It argued that people had a right to ask politicians 'to show some awareness of what they should be fighting about'. It went on:

> While it is true the people have to meet the huge bills contracted in their name by the politicians, they can find no satisfaction in whatever benefits they are paying for unless something else is added. That something is the idea of a future society which would be worth more effort to bring about than the British people seem willing to exert at present.
>
> Cakes and ale, even with free dyspeptic tablets thrown in, are not enough. What is needed is vision. Without vision the people perish. That is as true now as it was three thousand years ago . . . Contrary to what the politicians think, people are not so interested in free rides as they are to know where they are going.[2]

Now this was written at the time of a Labour Government.

But when Mr Heath eventually got into power and became Prime Minister it was just the same, or worse. By 1971 the problem had become a 'disease'. Once again *The Times'* leader had something to say. It was in a series on 'The Prospect of Britain'. Number 2 was headed, 'What is the British disease?' The conclusion was that it was a problem of a 'national psychology'. And the disease was 'depression'— not economic but spiritual:

> One of the failures of the 1960s has been that Britain has been treated as a purely materialist nation, and the treatment has not answered . . . What seems almost certain, however, is that the revival of national will which can restore Britain's economy cannot depend purely on economic motives. Some nations make civilization a by-product of the creation of wealth; Britain is more likely to make wealth a by-product of the creation of civilization.[3]

But when Mr Heath went from office and Mr Callaghan eventually became Prime Minister, did we see the problem go? Not a bit! At the end of Mr Callaghan's premiership, George Patterson was suggesting that the disease was in danger of becoming terminal! 'Can a dying Britain be saved?' was the title of his article on the state of the nation in 1979.

First he pointed out the 'physical symptoms': 50 million prescriptions a year for anti-anxiety drugs; attempted suicides rising from 30,000 in 1963 to about 100,000 in 1974 and rising at 10% per year; one million alcoholics (also increasing at an alarming rate) with another million problem drinkers.

But then he referred to the spiritual dimension. He quoted from Dostoyevsky's *Diary of a Writer*: 'An ethical idea has always preceded the birth of a nation . . . and when with the passage of time a nation's spiritual ideal is sapped, that nation falls, together with all its civil statutes and ideals.'[4]

But what about Mr Callaghan's successor, Mrs Thatcher?

What do we find? In May 1986, after seven years of her Government, Christie Davies, the Professor of Sociology at Reading University, implies that Britain's sickness is no longer a question of a terminal disease, since death has actually occurred! He wrote an article entitled *The strange death of moral England.*[5]

The crisis of values

In Homer's *Odyssey* we can read of how Odysseus was shipwrecked. But the first thing he did was to light a fire and cook a meal. Only then, when they had eaten, did the men remember their drowned companions and weep.

This primitive saga is so true to life. Physical needs take priority over emotional needs. But once the former are met, the deeper needs of human beings come to the surface. Gordon Rattray Taylor makes the important point: 'What happens on the personal scale can also happen on the world scale. The industrialised nations have now managed, broadly speaking, to provide their citizens with food, shelter and clothing. As a result, those citizens are becoming more aware of other and subtler needs.' But, he argues, these are not being met: 'We have scrambled out of physical poverty only to fall into psychological poverty. Indeed our condition is worse than poverty; we live in a psychological slum.'[6]

And this is the point that the Christian faith so emphatically makes. It follows the teaching of Jesus who said, quoting the Old Testament, 'Man shall not live by bread alone, but by every word that proceeds from the mouth of God' (Mt 4:4). So for this reason the deepest analysis of the state of the nation *must* engage with questions of value, and religious values at that. A fundamental failure, and a symptom of the problem, is to ignore this religious and spiritual dimension.

Even the Christian church is in danger of doing just that.

In February 1976 the General Synod of the Church of England debated the state of the nation. David Edwards had written a booklet for the debate. But the debate tended to focus on specific economic issues, such as employment, the humanization of industry and wage structures. Of course, the church ought to be concerned with those things. But the most profound *Christian* analysis of 'Britain's economic and social crisis' (as David Edwards described it at the time) could never be simply in terms of economics. To analyse the problems exclusively in terms of economics is the problem itself.

The trouble is, many people do believe that man at his most fundamental is no more than an economic animal. This reductionist view holds that the determining factors in man's behaviour, in the last analysis, are therefore economic. But the Christian gospel affirms that *that* belief is heresy, even though both the political left and right often share it. Marx propounded this view in one of its neatest forms. It is a measure of his success that the *assumption* behind his theory is now almost universal, often unacknowledged and even held among anti-Marxists! That is why Western politics seem to some observers little more than economics. Another dimension is required—shared values.

The need for shared values

In management thinking today the vital importance of 'shared values' is frequently stressed. They are essential for the success of any operation. On this subject Brian Griffiths, the head of Mrs Thatcher's 'Think Tank', quotes two works: *The Art of Japanese Management,* written by staff of the Harvard and Stanford Business Schools, and also *In Search of Excellence,* a study of the most successful American corporations undertaken jointly by an executive of McKinsey and Co. and a faculty member of Stanford. They show that the creation of shared values by management is crucial for explaining the success of leading US and Japanese companies.

McKinsey identified several key factors—to help us remember them they all begin with 'S'—structure, systems, skills, staff, style and shared values (or 'superordinate goals'!). Each is important, but shared values are essential. Shared values refer to 'the significant meanings', says Brian Griffiths, 'including spiritual values, to which an organization and its members devote themselves. Within the organization shared values integrate every other aspect of management decision-making and the shaping of values becomes the key role of top management.'[7] In support of this Thomas Watson Jr, the son of the founder of IBM wrote: 'I firmly believe that any organization, in order to survive and achieve success, must have a sound set of beliefs on which it premises all its policies and actions.'[8]

The same is true of nations. All groups—from the smallest to the largest nation-sized grouping—need healthy functioning in at least four areas (that is, if they are to be effective). First, there must be shared values, shared goals and an agreed agenda. There can be no way of reaching objectives and solving problems otherwise! Secondly, there needs to be competent leadership. You can never get beyond a poor leader. Thirdly, the structure of the group needs to be 'enabling' rather than obstructive. And fourthly, the group needs to relate to the total environment 'outside'. And it must relate in a way that is sympathetic and constructive.

All four areas are essential—values and goals; leadership; structures; and external relations. But of the four, values and goals have a precedence. *Nothing* can be achieved without agreement at this level. Weak leadership, poor structures or bad relationships outside the group can be fatal, but not always. But a lack of shared values and goals is nearly always fatal. For when you do not know where you are going or how to measure current performance, only extraordinary 'good luck' (or providence) can get you to the right destination.

This is true of a nation and it is also true of Britain. But currently there is a crisis of values. We are not agreed. In fact, with apparently some relish, people tell us that we are 'pluralistic'. And that is the real problem. For *at the most fundamental of levels 'pluralism' is an impossibility*.

The myth of pluralism

The thesis is simply this. At some point a society has to have *some* shared values and goals, otherwise it will tear itself apart. Happily, for many years, the truth of this has not been too self-evident. In part that is because we, along with other Western democracies, have been able to confine the 'combat' to debating chambers. As someone has suggested, politics is civil war conducted by other means. But there are sinister signs that *civil* 'civil-war' cannot go on for ever— witness the rise of terrorist activities and tactics on the one hand, and on the other hand, the violence that is being assumed by organized labour and by some of the protest movements, such as animal rights' groups. That the police in Britain are now committed to more drastic responses is part of the escalation.

It is all too easy to forget how 'fragile' a peaceful and humanitarian society really is. And such a society appears to go hand-in-hand with shared values. In Britain these have been the shared values of the Christian faith.

There is evidence to show that the current rise of violence and crime is not new, in the sense of being unprecedented. Rather, it is a reversion to the patterns of communal behaviour of earlier generations. Those more violent days were then followed by a time of strong shared values and beliefs (so it is argued); and this was an important factor in giving rise to a more peaceful social order.

The truth is that the period from 1890 to 1935 was quite

remarkable in terms of domestic 'peace and quiet'. And this was inspite of there being worse poverty, worse unemployment, worse slum living and worse educational opportunities than today. But these low figures and the recent rise in crime has meant that since the beginning of the century serious crimes have increased seventeen-fold![9]

Inevitably some of this may be due to better reporting and recording of crimes. But even the untrained in sociology are aware that they now have to use anti-burglary devices on their homes and property. If they are old enough, they can remember that in the past they never had to be so careful about locking property away. 'Things are not what they used to be'—in this respect at least.

Historical causation is never provable. But connections have to be considered. So what are some of the factors behind this period of good social order from 1890? One possible connection is that in the nineteenth century there was an earlier evangelical revival in the Christian church which produced a set of shared values. And this affected national values. That is to say, there were a sufficient number of people in the nation to make a difference who *together* felt that certain things were right and certain things were wrong. This in time had social and political implications.

Evangelical influence in the churches (the Church of England and the Free churches) in the nineteenth century was enormous. Its roots were in the earlier generation of John Wesley, John Whitefield and Charles Simeon. But by the time of the second half of the nineteenth century the revival had caused institutional change. By the end of the century, the period we are talking about, 50% of the Church of England was, at grass-roots level, evangelical. Parishes supporting the Church Missionary Society then numbered 5,700—nearly half the churches in the land (and the CMS was the evangelicals' missionary society). Why should it be so unreasonable to put this upsurge of vibrant Christian faith alongside a peaceful social order?

Then on top of the evangelical revival came the Tractarian movement and the revival in Christian social thinking generally. This produced some remarkable social thinkers such as Bishop Gore and William Temple. It also contributed to the many Christian social concerns that led to the Conference on Politics, Economics and Citizenship (COPEC) in 1924, and ultimately to the reforms that came to fruition during the Second World War and after, in the social legislation of the 1940s.

Lord Shaftesbury

The nineteenth-century evangelical revival is still instructive for today in terms of social change and direction. A clear example of the political effects of this revival is the case of Anthony Ashley Cooper, Lord Shaftesbury.[10] Too many have forgotten his legacy, and more importantly the reason for that legacy. For it was the Christian faith that motivated this great evangelical reformer.

Among other things Lord Shaftesbury had a strong conviction of eternity: 'There are not two hours in the day, but I think of the second advent of our Lord,' he said. Far from being an 'opiate', this conviction caused Shaftesbury to work for social change. In his own words, 'Christianity is not a speculation, it is essentially practical.'

The result was that Shaftesbury was able to reshape society in a more humane way. Apart from all the religious societies he was involved in, he was also vice-president (or patron) of the National Anti-Vivesection Society, the National Society for the Prevention of Cruelty to Children, and the Royal Society for the Prevention of Cruelty to Animals. Even at the level of humaneness and humanitarianism, let alone social justice, Shaftesbury's influence was remarkable.

Too often we take for granted our humanitarian heritage in the West (and indeed in the modern world generally). We forget how little humanitarianism counted in earlier ages of civilization. It was only in the nineteenth century that the world became 'civilized' in this respect. 'That [humanitarianism] began to count in Victorian times,' writes Martin Fagg, 'was due to the exertions of a comparatively few men and women. Outstanding among them was Anthony Ashley-Cooper, seventh Earl of Shaftesbury.'[11]

Humanitarian exertion was the story of Shaftesbury's career. His first move in practical (and political) Christianity was as the Chairman of the Lunacy Commission. Elected to Parliament at the age of twenty-five, two years later he was appointed to a Select Committee 'on pauper lunatics in the county of Middlesex and on Lunatic Asylums'. Shaftesbury was horrified at the treatment of the mentally ill. So in 1828 he seconded a bill to change the law. He then became the Chairman of the Lunacy Commission, developing an interest that was to last for over fifty years. As he wrote in his diary, 'So by God's blessing my first effort has been for the advancement of human happiness. May I improve hourly!'

He then had an interest in India. On appointment to the India Board he asked the question: 'India, what can I do for your countless myriads?' His answer was: 'There are two things, good government and Christianity.'

He, of course, saw these two things going hand in hand—politics and the Christian faith. And he suffered for allowing his Christianity to affect his politics. He was unpopular in Parliament when he successfully put an end to the custom of Sutteeism (the Indian custom of burning widows on their husbands' funeral pyres). He was unpopular for his support of the Ten Hours Bill. This Bill was part of the attack on inhuman conditions and hours experienced by children who worked in mills, mines and factories. It took fourteen years to pass the legislation! But he continually fought for the rights of children (including boy chimney sweeps), women and the poor.

His most significant work, perhaps, was in the Ragged School Union, which provided education for the poor. He was also involved in Public Health matters and was particularly concerned that there should be one day of rest a week. So he fought against required working on Sundays. Like his predecessors Hannah More and William Wilberforce, he was a great champion of the rights of working men and women.

Some say that in the 1840s and 1850s there was no revolution in England probably because of the work and witness of evangelical Christians! Guizot, Louis Philippe's premier, as a refugee in England said once to Shaftesbury, 'The religion alone of your country has saved you from revolution.' That evangelical legacy, when married to the tougher thinking on social and political affairs of some other Anglican traditions, produced a very remarkable mix—a shared set of values at a fundamental level. It is hard not to see this as having fruit in the peace and quiet of 1890 to 1935 and much of the good of our welfare state that was legislated for after the War.

It is vital, therefore, that we look back to men like Shaftesbury and more recently to men like William Temple. The social order they helped generate and that is still considered desirable cannot be explained apart from the Christian faith. Thus the new evangelicalism is a good omen.

Yet there are those who claim that while we have undoubtedly enjoyed this legacy, the Christian values no longer obtain; for we are a pluralist society.

3
Pluralism

Back in 1956 on the BBC Third Programme, Alasdair Mac-
Intyre, the philosopher-historian, gave a broadcast talk entitled 'A society without a metaphysics'. He said that the lack
of any beliefs in our society meant that it therefore lacked a
'glue'. This, he argued, was at the heart of our corporate and
cultural experience. 'The curious flavour that a combination
of liberal morality and metaphysical meaninglessness gives
to social life,' he suggested, 'is the characteristic flavour of
our time.'

The pluralist argument

Kenneth Leech, the Race Relations Field Officer for the
Board for Social Responsibility of the General Synod of the
Church of England, took up this theme in an article in *Third
Way* in 1982 entitled, 'The church in a plural society.'[1] He
wanted to assert, along with MacIntyre, that Britain could
no longer be called a 'Christian society'.

 The argument he used is probably familiar. But a sum-
mary needs to be made, as this is now taken by many as

axiomatic—that is, that Britain is 'pluralist' and no longer Christian.

His argument was as follows: organized Christianity is one of a number of minority groups within a post-Christian society. Christianity may have been important in shaping our past, but it is only of marginal importance in our present. The reality of this is most evident in the inner cities, for, he claims as many do (but against the evidence[2]), those 'urban cores' have never been Christianized since the Industrial Revolution. The irreligion of these urban areas will in time, he says, spread to suburbia, 'where church-going is still an accepted part of the mainstream culture'. True, there is still a 'decayed' form of vestigial Christianity in terms of 'folk religion' (or 'civic religion'), but that does not make a Christian culture.

However, Leech points to the fact that 'there is a considerable evidence of a resurgence of religions and faiths of various kinds'. We are not a secular culture. This is where the assessments of the sixties were wrong. The Chicago sociologist, Andrew Greeley, argued this in *The Persistence of Religion* in 1973:

> The religious needs of man have not changed since the late Ice Age. Secular man, technological man, man come of age, if he existed at all, only existed on university campuses, and increasingly only among the white, middle-aged senior faculty members, while the students indulged in astrology, the occult, and other cultic practices.

All this, Leech said, is true of Britain. Here we are seeing 'the *emergence* of new forms of religious expression, and, to a great extent, the *desperate* search for spiritual nourishment of the inner world'. There are five indicators: first, 'the black-led churches'; second, Eastern religions; third, 'private religions' (the occult, the 'new age' movement, meditation, magic and pagan revivals); fourth, 'fundamentalism'

(Leech here groups together fundamentalism in the mainstream churches, the Children of God, and Jehovah's Witnesses!); and fifth, Marxism ('it is impossible to discount the deeply religious element in modern Marxism').

All this is by now a fairly common analysis of modern Britain.

Not quite so simple

But is it quite so simple? What are the facts? What do people actually believe and want to identify with in terms of values?

The most detailed survey we have of beliefs and church allegiance in England is from the Bible Society and conducted by Gallup in October/November 1982.[3] The results were published by the Bible Society in 1983 as *Attitudes to the Bible, God and the Church*. The findings were interesting, particularly the answers to the question about religious and denominational affiliations. The answers, of course, were simply how the respondents saw themselves and were not necessarily supported by attendance or membership; but all had the option of saying, 'Don't know.' The percentages were as follows: 64%, Church of England; 11%, Roman Catholic; 7%, Methodist; 2%, Baptist; 1%, United Reformed; 1%, Jewish/Moslem/Hindu;[4] 7%, 'other'; 7%, 'Don't know'. That means *a total of 85% of the population think of themselves as Christian!* And that was just England; for the rest of the United Kingdom it is probably higher. A neutral observer therefore wouldn't immediately jump to the conclusion that Christianity was a minority concern in the way the pluralist argument suggests.

'But figures are deceptive,' someone says. 'Look at the figures quoted for the Church of England. That is quite unrealistic. Church attendance is infinitely lower.'

Matters are complicated. First, they are complicated by the fact that although the level of church commitment measured by attendance is seriously low and the institutional churches are in decline, *some* churches are growing significantly. This is true of all denominations. A recent Baptist survey has shown interesting patterns.[5] Secondly, the Bible Society survey showed that a total of 15% of the population consider themselves 'weekly' attenders (still eight million). But if you go to the overall category of 'any-time' church attenders—that is to discount those who only go for weddings or funerals, but to count those who attend once a year or more—you have 45% of the population.

Nevertheless, it is self-evident that in many of these cases we are not talking about 'a committed membership', 'born-again Christians', 'active workers', or whatever criterion you may choose for the heart of the Christian church. But you mustn't be too dismissive of the figures from surveys; for there are two kinds of statistics. To use the distinction of Peter Wagner, the authority on church growth at Fuller Theological Seminary in California, there are *World Christian Handbook* statistics—lists of everybody who would answer 'Christian' if a census-taker asked them to state their religion; but also there are the *Lamb's Book of Life* statistics. And the problem is this: while not all listed in the *World Christian Handbook* may be in the *Lamb's Book of Life,* the latter 'will not be available for publication until the final judgement day'. But sociologists 'have the *World Christian Handbook* in their libraries!'[6]

Sometimes we have to work with the tools available. And when we are dealing with the overall culture of a community and issues relating to the growth of the organizational church, *World Christian Handbook* statistics can be helpful.

Four dimensions

There is inevitably a difficulty in taking the spiritual temperature of a society. But part of this comes from a failure to perceive how the Christian church functions in relationship to its members and the total community. (And this is not only true of the Christian church. The dynamics could be paralleled in other religious groups that have a similar structural form.)

Broadly speaking, there are *four dimensions* to Christian experience that we must identify; and all are necessary for taking the spiritual temperature of a society. *First*, in terms of 'theological priority', there is the spiritual transformation of the individual. This must involve an encounter with God —that experience of what Rudolf Otto called 'a tremendous and fascinating mystery'. This then leads to the desire for personal forgiveness and reconciliation with God, new life, strength and spiritual power—in fact the desire and the need to be 'born again'. This is an over-used phrase, but it is essentially accurate and with the imprimatur of Jesus! There is thus the need for the spiritual transformation of individuals and their spiritual nurture. Much of traditional Christianity deals with this.

Second, the Christian faith is about 'the people of God'. Christianity is essentially a corporate experience. St Paul wrote eloquently about the body of Christ, with many limbs and parts making up one whole. This went alongside the notion of the *ecclesia*, the assembly, the called-out ones. The result is that the Christian faith can never be fully understood nor fully experienced apart from a community of faith and a community of the faithful. And the *ecclesia* (translated in our Bibles as 'church') is a society distinct from the world that is 'outside'. So this includes all we mean by the Christian congregation and all the paraphernalia of parish and church life—pastoral care of the members, worship, teaching, giving, local leadership and (sooner or later) buildings.

However, the *third* dimension of Christian experience relates to the other side of the life of the church—the universal side. For each church is a manifestation of the 'one, holy, catholic and apostolic church'. The picture is complicated theologically and practically. This is because the local church is not just a branch, like the bank on the high street. It has a completion in itself. But, nevertheless, it is still only part of the universal church, with which it is in fellowship. So Christianity will always have an 'extra-parochial' expression.

Currently this is seen in national and international denominational organizations; in 'para-church' organizations (these include such diverse bodies as the Roman Catholic monastic orders and evangelistic agencies like Campus Crusade for Christ); and in ecumenical and interdenominational organizations. Even the newer house churches that argue against the existence of denominations end up with 'associations', 'links' or 'coverings' that look suspiciously like embryonic denominations!

The public realm

The *fourth* dimension of Christian experience has great, but often unnoticed, significance. This relates to the relationship of the church with the environment around, that is to say, to the society of men and women and the structures that hold this society together—its politics, culture, values, beliefs, aims and 'axioms' (which we will discuss later): this is the 'public realm', in fact. And it is in this public realm in Britain that we have a religious establishment; and that establishment is very strong because of the establishment in the nation of the Church of England and the Church of Scotland.

Legally, with regard to the Church of England, establishment means very little. All it means is that the state has accepted the Church of England as a Christian body and given to it a certain legal position. Part of that legal position allows Parliament a veto on Measures that the General Synod passes. But those Measures account for only a small amount of the Synod's business. And Parliament only rarely exercises its rights. And even then, because it is the more committed Christian MPs who attend the debates, Parliament's veto can be good for the Church! Certainly its Ecclesiastical Committee has a useful legislative function in stimulating the Church to produce good and fair legislation without omissions and inconsistencies.

However, the real significance of the Church of England's establishment is its effects—bishops sitting in the House of Lords being only one. More significantly, the establishment affects the whole psychology of the nation. Through various legal settlements and traditional forms for state and public occasions, the Church of England is intimately bound up with our public life. This affects the 'flavour' of the nation. So, far from the nation having a flavour of being without a 'metaphysic', at this corporate level—in this fourth dimension—the nation is *highly* 'metaphysical', for it is positively Christian. This is supremely illustrated by the British monarchy.

Britain does not have a written constitution but an evolved national constitution; and what has evolved is overtly Christian. For the constitution is held together by the Crown. But the British monarch is both head of state *and* Governor of the Church of England. In this way, whether we like it or not, the sovereign symbolizes Christian values as being the official values of the nation. They are woven into our national system. And this is more than just a question of flavour. It is both a legal *and* a liturgical reality, and thus structurally part of the fabric of the public realm in Britain. How is this?

We need to look at the Coronation Service. The present Queen of Britain, Elizabeth II, has had a long reign. So the phenomenon of Coronation can easily be forgotten. But in April 1986, a month we have already referred to, Her Majesty the Queen celebrated her sixtieth birthday; and she used it as an opportunity for remembering her Coronation.

One of her most pointed references that month was to her Coronation Oath. She wanted to reaffirm her commitments made on June 2nd, 1953 (interestingly only three years before Alasdair MacIntyre said we were a 'society without a metaphysic').

What were those commitments? They are enshrined in the Coronation Service and especially in the Coronation Oath.

The Coronation of Queen Elizabeth II

The questions the then Archbishop of Canterbury asked the Queen in the early fifties were set out in the Order of Service drawn up for the occasion.[7] These were statutory questions.

Archbishop: Will you solemnly promise and swear to govern the Peoples of the United Kingdom of Great Britain and Northern Ireland, Canada, Australia, New Zealand . . . and of your Possessions and the other Territories to any of them belonging or pertaining, according to their respective laws and customs?
Queen: I solemnly promise so to do.
Archbishop: Will you to your power cause Law and Justice, in Mercy, to be executed in all your judgements?
Queen: I will.
Archbishop: Will you to the utmost of your power maintain the Laws of God and the true profession of the Gospel? Will you to the utmost of your power maintain in the United Kingdom the Protestant Reformed Religion established by law? Will you maintain and preserve inviolably the settlement of the Church of England, and the doctrine, worship, discipline, and government thereof, as by law established in England? Will you preserve unto the Bishops and Clergy of England, and to the Churches there committed to their charge, all such rights and privileges, as by law do or shall appertain to them or any of them?
Queen: All this I promise to do.

And immediately after this solemn oath, the Moderator of the General Assembly of the Church of Scotland, the other great Established Church in Britain, presented the Queen with a Bible, and said these words:

> Our gracious Queen: to keep your Majesty ever mindful of the Law and the Gospel of God as the Rule for the whole life and government of Christian Princes, we present you with this Book, the most valuable thing that this world affords.

And the Moderator continued:

> Here is Wisdom; this is the royal Law; these are the lively Oracles of God.

Later on there was the presentation of the traditional 'regalia', including the Orb. This was presented to the Queen by the Archbishop with these words: 'Receive this Orb set under the Cross, and remember that the whole world is subject to the Power and Empire of Christ our Redeemer.'[8]

The constitution

The Coronation service is of great significance both for constitutional government and parliamentary democracy. It also gives a Christian basis to our society. It ensures supremely that the Queen is a *Christian* and a *constitutional* monarch. In it she assents to the British constitution and to the role of Christianity in the public life of the United Kingdom.

The Christian, constitutional and Parliamentary character of the monarchy was settled once and for all by the Revolution of 1689. That meant that the monarch was and is to abide by church and state law. It is a constitutional (or 'conferred' monarchy), not a 'hereditary' (or automatic) one—as Edward VIII had to discover.

The British monarchy normally devolves from the holder to the monarch's heir, but it is not an absolute right. James II was King by hereditary right. William and Mary, however, became King and Queen because the Crown was conferred on them by Parliament. This was done because they agreed to accept the Declaration of Rights set out in an Act of 1689.

The Act at the same time said that the Sovereign should always be of the 'Protestant Religion'. Another Act in the same year introduced a form of the Coronation Oath to fit in with these arrangements. So that is why our Queen needed to agree to promise to uphold the Protestant Religion, and needed to promise to 'govern . . . according to their respective laws and customs'. This is at the heart of the Oath. And it is Parliament and the General Synod of the Church of England that decides the 'laws and customs' according to which the Queen has agreed to govern the nation and the Church of England.

An Act passed in 1701 required that the monarch had not only to be Protestant but an Anglican; an Act passed in 1707 stipulated that the monarch had 'to maintain and preserve inviolably the settlement of the Church of England'. The net result of all this is that the British monarch is to be a professing *Christian*. So because of these constitutional arrangements and safeguards it is very hard to call Britain a 'plural' society.

But the picture is complicated. Constitutionally—at a structural level—we are undoubtedly a Christian country and there is also a large amount of 'professed' Christian allegiance. But people are not going to church. That leads some to argue that there must be a great dichotomy between the two types of statistics Peter Wagner refers to in terms of the British experience; it leads others to say that we are a 'plural' society and in no way Christian.

But we have to be careful. We need to assess the nation under the four dimensions or categories outlined above. For it is possible and necessary to analyse both Christianity *and* the wider society from the perspective of the individual, the local church, wider church structures and national culture and public life. You then find a complex picture.

For example, it is possible to be a deeply spiritual Christian individual, but to be in a very shallow local church. You can have a thriving local church, but its individual members may be spiritually weak. You can have 'live' individuals and churches within 'dead' wider church structures and denominations. You can have stimulating wider church structures, but some of the local manifestations can be depressing (this is particularly true with some para-church organizations). And it is possible to have a national culture that is Christian (in part at least) when many of the nation's citizens have individually questionable Christian allegiance.

Society and the individual

There is nothing particularly odd about there being a stronger level of public Christian allegiance and aspiration than the level of private Christian allegiance. Societal goals are often higher than individual achievement. This is true of the whole legal system.

That doesn't mean to say that this divergence or any divergence between teaching and practice or goals and performance is good. Far from it. Indeed, having the 'form of religion but denying its power', according to Christian understanding, is never good. It is hypocrisy! But that doesn't mean to say we should either despise, disregard or seek to destroy the form. Rather, we ought to seek the power! True righteousness has to *exceed* that of the Pharisees. Jesus said that although we are not to do as they do, we are to do what they teach (Mt 23:3). All this is to be applied to individual life, congregational life, denominational life and public life.

But the question that has faced us for much of this century, following the waning of the nineteenth-century evangelical revival and the decline of other traditions, is this: how long can you maintain healthy functioning, either in the church or in the nation, if there is a radical failure in any one of the 'four dimensions'? The crisis Kenneth Leech points to

45

is the crisis of the congregation. Christian congregational life is currently very weak in the United Kingdom. And congregations are weak both because the wider structures (all that goes to make denominational life) are weak and because individual faith needs reviving and renewing.

There clearly is a limit as to how far you can sustain a Christian culture when the church is failing. But the current failure of the churches and the attendant spiritual weakness of individual Christians doesn't automatically allow us to say that public life in Britain has ceased to be Christian. In many respects it has. In many respects it has not; for legal and constitutional enactments, whether we like it or not, do affect the culture.

And so many, according to the statistics, want to identify with the Church of England and the other Trinitarian churches. This indicates that in some measure they assent to the Christian shape of British corporate life and culture. If, then, these large percentages are showing preferences, what right have others to deny or obstruct these preferences? Yet that is what is perceived to be happening.

Indeed this is serious. There are constitutional means, via Parliament, of corporately changing the religious flavour of our nation. But until that is done the flavour *must* remain Christian. Patronizing elites—whether in the media or in education—who unilaterally decide to impose their values need to be resisted. To date this has not adequately been done. Therefore subtly, without any referendum, certain minorities have been restructuring values. Of course, if there was ever a constitutional majority who wanted to reject Christian values in public life, the church would be obliged to show how misjudged and disastrous such a position was. But it would then have to accept it.

Until then, the church should not only teach but assert Christian values in the Public Square. Of course, private conscience must always be respected, as must minority groupings. There can never be intolerance of individuals. But neutrality is impossible. For the secular humanism that is being imposed by the backdoor is also a *religion*. It is not 'value free'. And constitutionally the United Kingdom is not secular humanist but Christian!

The quip that 'the creed of the English is that there is no God, and that it is wise to pray to him from time to time' is witty but, according to the evidence, untrue. We are not a nation of born-again believers. But there are probably more God-fearers than the advocates of the plural society admit. And the majority of these God-fearers, in so far as the figures show, seem to want a Christian social order.

4

The Public Square

In recent decades, 'pluralism' has become something of a buzz-word. It is variously employed. Often it is used to argue that no normative ethic even of the vaguest and most tentative sort, can be 'imposed' in our public life. In practice it means that public policy decisions reflect a surrender of the normal to the abnormal, of the dominant to the deviant.

So writes Richard Neuhaus in a very important study, *The Naked Public Square.*[1]

The real facts

He cites an interesting example from his own experience. It illustrates how we can easily be seduced into assuming that the marginal is normative. We then claim we are a plural society.

Fairly recently in the United States there was a White House Conference on Families. Neuhaus, an American, was asked to serve on the working party. The group was under considerable pressure from activist homosexual and feminist organizations. They argued that the sixties and seventies had so revolutionized sexual behaviour that we now needed to adopt new ways of defining the family. These groups were wanting changes in the law to reflect this. In an exchange with a gay activist spokesman the Conference tried to be specific as to what was *really* going on in terms of sexual behaviour.

The spokesman, a doctor, agreed that the US Government's legitimate concern was not so much in regulating sexual relationships as in protecting children. He agreed, too, for the sake of the argument, with the considerable overestimate that 10% of the population might be homosexual. That would be 25 million Americans. When questioned the doctor said that his organization reckoned that of that figure 20% would be exclusively homosexual in orientation and actively homosexual in practice—that is, five million 'gays'. There was agreement, too, on a five-year 'longevity test' for relationships, since 'one-night stands' could obviously not qualify as a family unit. The doctor's informed guess was that five per cent of homosexual couples had lived together for five years or more. That gave 125,000 'married couples'. But how many of these would have the care of children or elderly dependants? Again, he thought about five per cent. But that only gave 6,250 homosexual 'families' that were of any concern to government policy.

The doctor's figures, it was said, may have been greatly inflated. But even had they been accurate, 'in a society of more than 230 million people the revolution he and others declare is an almost imperceptible ripple'. Of course, it was acknowledged that even a mere few hundred people are important for public policy for the sake of children and dependants. But 'that a national commission should spend millions of dollars recommending the overhaul of family law in America on the basis of such "revolutions" is, not to put too fine a point on it, absurd'.[2]

A weird logic or 'theology' is at work. The concern for the

marginal and minorities is rooted in the Judaeo-Christian tradition. The Bible shows a concern for orphans, widows, the fatherless, and 'the stranger within the gates'. The result is that terms such as 'minorities' and 'the marginal' have high moral status. But, says Neuhaus,

> when such mandates to benevolence are legalistically codified
> . . . the claims of those who deviate from the moral consensus constitute a powerful leverage against the consensus that gives moral status to the claims in the first place. Thus it is asserted that one who deviates has the 'right' not to be affected, at least in public, by the beliefs, symbols, and rules of the majority culture . . . The protection of an 'alternative life-style' such as homosexuality turns heterosexual marriage into just another 'alternative life-style'. In this way, the Judaeo-Christian ethic, when legalistically implemented, works against itself; the morally mandated respect for the marginal assures that the centre cannot hold.[3]

And Neuhaus' conclusion is this: 'What is frequently meant by pluralism today is a legalised secular distortion of Judaeo-Christian concern for the marginal.'[4]

Toleration

A Christian society must not be an 'intolerant' society. Indeed the English constitution is both Christian and tolerant. The Act of Toleration in 1688, the repeal of the Test and Corporation Acts in 1828 and Catholic Emancipation in 1829 meant that the law or the constitution would not enforce religious belief or practice. Of course, with any 'toleration' a pluralism of views is being recognized.

But in the United Kingdom this pluralism has evolved as a 'subordinate' pluralism, derived from a prior belief that toleration is right. But this belief is part of the inherited Judaeo-Christian tradition where God, in his mercy, is active to save and restore mankind, but not at the expense of human freedom. Man is always free to reject God and his will. That is what the Christian doctrine of hell guarantees. God, in Christ, does all he can to block man's downward path. But if a man or woman so chooses, God will allow him the freedom to reject him.

Because of this fundamental Christian doctrine, toleration allowing human freedom is integral to the Christian faith. Thus a society based on Christian values will inevitably have a subordinate pluralism. Indeed a case can be argued for saying that pluralism is the product of a Christian culture. But such a pluralism must not be construed as meaning there is no 'super-ordinate' or primary set of unifying (not plural) beliefs or values—beliefs or values that are normative and constitutive for the community. Indeed, there must be if there is to be any meaningful community within which pluralism is a possibility.

We have already seen that shared values and goals are essential in any grouping if it is to cohere. But at the moment we are experiencing a crisis over these shared values and goals in Britain. The danger then is this: minority views and values, in the absence of ones that are commonly agreed, fill the vacuum. But this will be at the cost of serious resentment. For when majorities find that views and values are being imposed in society by minorities or sub-cultures, there is a danger of a backlash. Instead of peaceful pluralism you have strife—anything from moral strife to racial strife.

This crisis in shared values is in no small part due to the fact that for too long the believing and active Christian constituency in the nation has been too quiet in the public realm. It has assumed that our society is pluralistic in a basic sense and so has reckoned it has no *right* to share its views. But this is a failure to respond to its duties. In a nation with a Christian sub-structure, the church has a duty. Certainly it is not a duty to force its beliefs on those who do not want to respond; but it is a duty to articulate, teach and reinforce the beliefs

51

that undergird the common and public life of the nation. A failure to do that cannot be justified as respecting the integrity of others; rather it is to be condemned as evacuating the Public Square and leaving it empty. But the Public Square cannot remain empty in a state of benign liberalism. As in the parable of Jesus, when the house is left vacant demons worse than before invade! What is true of the individual is true of the nation. There cannot be a spiritual vacuum. Neutrality is not an option.

And this is being sensed at large. There is a new mood abroad. There is a yearning for 'authority' and for guidance. It is a world-wide phenomenon and is seen most obviously in Britain in the evangelical renaissance we have referred to that is taking place within all the churches. This is usually called a 'conservative' development, not to be confused with a politically conservative development. Many younger evangelicals have left wing sympathies.

A parallel is often drawn with conservative religious movements in other countries, cultures and even faiths. But in the United Kingdom the evangelical renaissance is uniquely British, educated and politically moderate. In the United States it is more 'populist', but far more sophisticated politically—already it has produced two Presidents. In Islamic states, or those that are trying to become such, it hardly needs to be said that Muslim fundamentalism is extremely powerful.

Authority

But it would be very foolish to extrapolate from all the religious movements in the world and then try to 'read off' some common factor. For, in reality, the Moral Majority of the United States and the Muslim Brotherhood share little in common. Furthermore, British evangelical Christianity is very different from the Moral Majority in the United States.

But there is one thing in common that all these movements have, and that is a rejection of secularism in all its forms. That is what is happening world-wide. We are coming to the end of an era of secularism.

If so, these religious movements are in the van of a world-wide cultural shift. This means that around the world the question of religion and the questions from religion are now coming centre-stage. The cry is for authority; and after experiments this century with this-worldly human authorities in the form of totalitarian oppressors (Stalin, Hitler, Mao), the cry is for a more transcendent form of authority—an authority that doesn't simply validate and justify the status quo or social order, which may possibly be hideous and inhuman. What is wanted is an authority that can 'judge' and direct the social order.

'But isn't this a regression to a puerile mentality—the cry for authority in life?' someone will ask. No! We have to make distinctions. Following Neuhaus,[5] we need to distinguish between what is 'authoritarian', 'autonomous' and 'authoritative'. To want security in an authoritarian person or structure is immature or puerile. It is the security of being told what to do without option. It is easy, but involves no personal input. Sooner or later it will cause a reaction and a desire for release from the 'authoritarian' into a more 'autonomous' mode, where we are our own masters and enjoy freedom and liberty.

But absolute freedom or autonomy is a bondage itself. Like a jelly without a mould, it is very hard to handle. True fulfilment comes not when we are totally unrestrained and aimless, but when we *freely* choose to follow a path or a destiny. Submission to what is recognized as rightly *authoritative* (because its worth has been proved) is the mark of maturity.

A number of observers see this movement from the authoritarian to the autonomous and then to the authoritative as taking place in our culture at large. For two hundred years we thought we had arrived, and that 'man had come of age'. But that period of optimism is coming to an end. We realize the need for more than our own freedom. We want guidelines so that we can use our freedom constructively. That is why, in terms of the social order, we need the Christian voice to be heard again and to be heard distinctly.

But for too long the Public Square has been without that voice. Without any conspiracy, assumptions have been made that have led the religious contender to feel unwanted in public. 'Religion is for the private realm, not the public,' it is said. The result has been *secularism*. This has had a debilitating effect on our national life. No one has ever voted that this should be so. It has just happened. And it is dangerous. Once you have a truly secular social order you are one step from totalitarianism. Obviously, if religion is excluded from the public arena, all you are left with is the state and the individual. Religion is no longer available to check the ambitions of the state!

The challenge to the church

The wars of religion in seventeenth-century Europe—conflicts of competing 'authoritarianisms'—were examples of exhausting and fanatical passions. They drained the continent. Afterwards many were absolutely determined to keep religion out of public life. This led to the formation of the secularist and autonomous doctrines of the eighteenth-century Englightenment. The secularist philosophies of today are descended from that cultural phenomenon.

But secularism has now run its course. The world has been exhausted by a set of autonomous passions, more terrible than the authoritarian ones. The militant secularism of Hitler, Stalin and Mao has caused infinitely worse devastation than was ever caused by the extremes of European religious fanaticism. In three hundred years of the Inquisition, it has been reckoned, there were fewer people killed than on any one afternoon during the period of Stalin's purges and Hitler's concentration camps.

We are now in a new age when there is a realization that some transcendent meaning *has* to be given to life on this planet; but it needs to be well founded, arguable and true. The serious danger Western society and indeed the world faces at the moment is this: because the Public Square is empty, it is a prey to any of the competing ideologies that are in the market-place. The modern technology of mass manipulation through the media means that the consequences of false ideologies are grave. Any fanatic—not necessarily religious—given the funding, is capable of misleading millions. We face the possibility of the realization in a very modern way of the prophecy of Jesus that 'false Christs' would come and lead many astray. There is an urgency, therefore, for the Christian church to share more emphatically and less apologetically its gospel of God's love and God's grace through the cross and resurrection of Jesus Christ.

But what is the church to do? John Stott in his book, *Issues Facing Christians Today,* outlines three possible responses for the Christian in the modern world in helping to shape or reshape values. First, there is the 'imposition' of views on others. He cites the Inquisition and Prohibition as two examples of this approach.

> Looking back at these two examples, one European and the other American, the Inquisition was an attempt to impose belief, and Prohibition an attempt to impose behaviour. Both were seen in the end to be unproductive, for you cannot force people to believe what they do not believe, or practise what they do not want to practise. Similarly, to imagine today that we can force Christian convictions and standards on Europe is totally unrealistic. It is a foolish nostalgia for a Christendom which has long since vanished.[6]

55

Secondly, there is the attitude of *laissez-faire,* and by this he means 'a mood of apathy and indifference . . . Far from propagating our views, we say, we will not even propagate or commend them.' He cites the German churches' failure to speak out against Hitler as the most glaring and dreadful recent example of this attitude. 'The complicity of the "German Christians" [to be distinguished from the German "Confessing Church"], who failed to develop a biblical critique of the Nazis' blatant racism, should be enough to outlaw laissez-faire forever.'[7]

Persuasion

The third response is that of 'persuasion'. It acknowledges the character of God. Unlike the attitude of *laissez-faire,* it takes seriously what God takes seriously—righteousness, justice and the needy. But it also acknowledges the character of man as a responsible, free individual, whose conscience is to be respected. And this, says Stott, is the Christian way. 'We therefore need doctrinal apologetic in evangelism (arguing the truth of the gospel) and ethical apologetic in social action (arguing the goodness of the moral law). Apologists of both kinds are wanted urgently in today's church and world.'[8] Most people in the churches today would agree with John Stott. Of that there can be no doubt.

But the vitally important question that then needs to be asked is this: 'Precisely of what and where should Christians be persuading the world in our present situation?'

The answer to the question 'where', in our context, is obvious; they should be exercising their skills of persuasion in the Public Square. But the answer to the question 'what' is not so obvious.

For a long time the practice of the churches suggests that the Christian in the Public Square should give 'second order' comment. This is the result of Christians working out the *implications* of the gospel (as regards social and political affairs), and then translating them into specific pronouncements that are meant to be heard by government and opposition parties.

It works in practice like this. You start with 'first order' beliefs—for example, that God is love, that he is the Almighty Creator, that *all* mankind has been created in his image, that God has revealed his will through prophets and apostles in the Bible and supremely in Christ, that Christ is the Redeemer, that Christ has shown disease and poverty to be the enemy, that the future is important as well as the present and the past (for we shall all have to stand before the judgement seat of Christ), that death is not the end and that this world is not all there is. Then from these and other first order beliefs there arise a host of social and political implications, and these are of interest to people outside the church. For example, there is a 'bias to the poor', a concern for freedom, a concern for the future of the planet, a concern for the human, a concern for personal morality, and so on. So Christians then speak on these second order issues in the Public Square. And that is good.

But that is not the primary contribution that the world at the moment needs to hear. The Public Square is not totally devoid of second order moralizing or advice. What it lacks are first order beliefs that can ground or justify these various political and social ideals and options. And in Britain this lack is due to insufficient intelligent proclamation and persuasion by the churches concerning fundamental beliefs. So what needs to be heard in the Public Square more than anything else is a statement about reality that deals with ultimate truth and meaning. People actually do want to hear the truth about God, man and the world, as taught by Jesus; and this must be heard in the Public Square!

The task

The Queen was told at her Coronation to 'remember that the whole world is subject to the Power and Empire of Christ our Redeemer'. That is not a pietistic truth. It is a truth of political and social importance. Christ is Lord of all or he is not Lord at all! That many do not realize its importance is why persuasion is needed. But the fact that politically it may not yet be universally acknowledged by itself proves little. Few countries are yet persuaded of the value of democracy. Of the 159 members of the United Nations, probably less than thirty qualify as democracies. But we do not believe democracy has no value for that reason!

So the wider world needs to hear from the church not just second order prescriptions, but first order premises on which those prescriptions are based and against which they can be judged and evaluated. Otherwise you have the pathetic spectacle of senior clergy, politicians, media people and other opinion formers simply following the latest fashion in sympathies.

There is abroad a simplistic but not altogether illegitimate notion that the church's business is to talk about religion rather than politics! People look to the church for meaning, direction and an overview of the social order. Of course, they are wrong to think that the church should never help people see the implications of that meaning and *never* talk about politics. But they are right in feeling cheated if the church does not help them at this deepest point of need and if it seems to be preoccupied with detailed political policies and solutions.

And being more in the Public Square doesn't necessarily mean being more involved in politics. Public affairs are not co-terminous with government affairs. Politicians are not the only people to inhabit the Public Square. There is a great deal that is public that is not political. Some Christians seem to think, however, that to be involved in political debate is the only way to make Christianity more relevant to public life. But family life, work, sport, entertainment, leisure activities and education can all be very public matters.

The reason why we believe politics is more public than some other areas of life is partly because of current media practice. Our world of experience today impinges on us through the filter of professional communicators, as we shall be seeing later. They interpret reality for us. But they, like many of us in the West, are (in Neuhaus' phrase) 'victims of secularizing mythology'. Yet these people are, to a degree, determiners of what counts as public and real. For the 'news' that is presented to us is the result of prior judgements. Currently it is judged that 'news' is (in the West) politics first and foremost, and then scandal, disasters and accidents.

It is to be noticed that in this scheme of things 'religion' in its own right seldom impinges on the public, except when there is a scandal—for example, clerical immorality, clerical heresy or the possibility of a church split. For the rest, religion is confined to 'God-slots' on radio and television, either early in the morning, when most people are still not awake, or late at night, when most people have gone to bed.

However, there is a perceptible change, particularly in the 'quality' press. Religion is becoming news in its own right even without scandal. It is perhaps not without significance that in 1986 a major award in journalism went to the Religious Correspondent of *The Times,* Clifford Longley.

But because of the power of these 'interpreting elites' there is a knock-on effect as far as the church is concerned. For when the Christian church addresses itself to any question of public concern, there is a danger. Richard Neuhaus describes it as accepting 'the framing of the question without reference to anything specifically religious. [The church] is pleased to be admitted as a guest to the public debate and takes care to behave by the rules prescribed by the host. This perhaps unconscious collaboration with secularism's agenda was reflected in the 1960s slogan of some ecumenical agencies, "The world sets the agenda for the Church."[9]

5
Aims and Axioms

Any society needs to be analysed from three perspectives—the political, the economic and the religious or moral-cultural perspectives. It is one of the failures of the West that for too long 'public affairs' have been equated with the political and economic. But the major problems being faced today are not so much in the area of either politics or economics but in the areas of morals, culture and religion—in fact, in the realm of the spirit.

Decline and fall

The oil crisis in the aftermath of the Arab-Israeli war of 1975 created near panic in the West. It coincided with an increase of terrorism and violence. There were all sorts of analyses attempted in terms of politics and economics. It caused a great deal of heart searching about life, the direction of society and values. But among the most perceptive were the comments of the Chief Rabbi, Dr Immanuel Jakobovits:

> I cannot believe that the civilized world as we knew it is inevitably coming to grief and ruin in a convulsion of unprecedented

proportions, simply because some effective political and economic formulae have eluded us and the requisite wisdom has suddenly failed our statesmen and their select teams of skilled advisors and efficient bureaucrats.

Past civilizations did not decline and fall simply because some inept heads made the wrong decisions in moments of crisis, but because of the ailments afflicting the body of society, largely in the intangible domain of the soul and spirit . . . There can be no brotherhood of man without the Fatherhood of God. It is only as children of a common God that we humans are brothers. Take away the link in the chain of human fraternity and understanding disintegrates. Dethrone God and the dignity of man . . . created in His image is bound to collapse.[1]

This is the distinctly Judaeo-Christian analysis of the dilemma, not just of 1973-1975 but of today. And it speaks of the possibility of the *decline of Western Civilization*—no less.

But what do we mean by 'Western Civilization' or 'Western Culture'? Most people mean by these terms the liberal stage of Western development. To talk about a decline, of course, is to say that it was a good development. It is to suggest that the liberal values were essentially worth while. And most of us would agree with that. It is hard to deny that much of what has emerged from the Enlightenment and the age of reason is positive and good. The age has now turned sour; certainly it was deficient in its awareness of God; and in the end it may be seen that the age has caused much long-term harm. But it would be foolish to ignore and lose all that was good and all that led to genuine progress. No one wants to regress now to another dark age! Rather, a salvage operation is required. This is imperative. For it is by no means impossible that the West could wander into a new barbarism.

But if there is decline in the West, how has it happened? How, in fact, does a culture or a civilization decline? To answer that question I want to take up the notion of *aims* and *axioms* used by V. A. Demant, in his Scott Holland Lectures of 1949, entitled *Religion and the Decline of Capitalism*. I need to elaborate his arguments; for if we can see his distinction between aims and axioms, I believe that it will help us to understand the mechanics of cultural and social change and our own predicament. We can then more easily map out where we are.

Aims and axioms

First, what do we mean by 'aims'? Simply this: these are the views people hold about the 'good life'—the things they want to be and do, the possessions they want to have, the system they want to live under; it is, in fact, the way of life they reckon desirable and are willing to spend time, energy and money on. But these aims are to be seen not only in terms of individual and personal goals, but in terms of the aspirations of a whole age or period.

Secondly, what do we mean by 'axioms'? These are the *presuppositions* people have. They relate to the wider questions of life and existence. They are the 'background beliefs' that people hold about the nature of the world, man and his place in society. They may be held almost unconsciously. They are rather like the air you breathe; you are not aware of it until it is no longer there!

Now, these axioms may be expressed as doctrines or ideologies. They can then be taught, discussed or preached. But it is possible that they are most influential when they are not formulated at all. Rather, they are *assumed*. They then become the datum that gives rise to various doctrines and ideas. But we must note this: in our society these axioms themselves are dependent on certain fundamental beliefs such as you get in the Christian faith. That is why some have called these 'middle axioms'. They stand half-way between social aims and religious beliefs.

Now what is needed for cultural growth and vitality is simply this: the aims of a society need to be backed up by its axioms, so that the axioms then reinforce the aims. But if aims are being held that are no longer backed up by a society's current axioms, you have cultural decline and decay. And, of course, the decline in religion in time will affect these axioms, giving a knock-on effect. True, when religious belief declines, the axioms it produces can remain for a period; and when these axioms decline, the aims can remain for a period. But you cannot maintain your aims for ever without supporting middle axioms and religious beliefs.

This, in outline, is Demant's general theory. But how does it work out in detail? As a preliminary we must recognize a *general* aim of Western democratic liberal culture—freedom and an absence of state interference. Demant remarks:

> The aims of liberalism have been to embody in life and thought the truth that while man is a social being, he does not exist merely for the social whole. He has certain valid *human* goals, such as the pursuit of knowledge, the creation of civilization, the exercise of each one's proper skills, the enrichment of personal life and relations and the fulfilment of spiritual destiny.[2]

So there must be a limit to state interference to ensure this freedom. This was John Stuart Mill's point in his essay *On Liberty*:

> There is a limit to the legitimate interference of collective opinion with individual independence, and to find that limit and to maintain it against encroachment is as indispensable to the good condition of human affairs as protection against political despotism.[3]

This, then, is a general aim of what we can describe as Western liberal culture. But what are some of its *specific* aims? Straightaway we can identify three. They are important because we could easily mistake them as being permanent aspects of human society and existence, when they certainly are not.

Truth, right and wrong

First, in Western democratic liberalism there is the aim of 'pursuing truth', as we conventionally understand it as related to the scientific method. But there is nothing automatic about the pursuit of truth! You only have an honest search or exploration, and with agreed methods of testing hypotheses, when there is the prior assumption (or axiom) that there is an objective reality that calls for exploration, that appears to be analysable, that invites investigation (without bias and as disinterestedly as possible) and there is both the predictable and the unpredictable in nature.

Yet this middle axiom depends on something like the prior Christian understanding of man and the world—that this world is the arena both of God's normal 'regular' working and of his miraculous intervention; and man stands in relation to the external world as fundamentally a creature and not as Creator. His own ideas, plans and activities do not determine reality. They are reactions to what is given or the reordering of what is already there. So man, the world and God are differentiated. God is real and not just a figment of man's imagination. The world is real. It is not all in flux. It behaves in a reasonably predictable way; yet testing of theories about it is required, because not everything that happens is predictable. And it is objective.

All that may seem so obvious. However, it is a phenomenon of the modern world that some people, having lost a belief in the living God, have ceased to believe in the world as a knowable objective reality. So a belief in the relativity of all things is not uncommon. The existentialism that has influenced a number of modern liberal theologians is a good example. So this approach to knowledge is found even in the church. The recent debate over fundamental doctrine in the

Church of England—regarding the Virgin Birth and the Empty Tomb of Jesus—can be seen in part as a clash between two theories of knowledge. One is the traditional Christian one that treats objective truth as possible; the other is more secularist and sees truth as less objective and more 'man-conditioned'. Demant gives a caricature of this relativist approach to knowledge (or epistemology) in this epigram: 'There is no truth, scientific, cultural or religious that is not propaganda in some form or another.'[4]

So here you have the first aim—the pursuit of truth. The axiom or the assumption is that there is an objective reality to explore and find out about. But that axiom is related to the Christian belief in God as Creator and man as creature.

A second aim of Western democratic liberalism is for society to be able to call some things 'right' and other things 'wrong'. This aim means, as Demant says, that 'good is an attribute of a certain kind of life and cannot be identified with life itself or with the bare success of an act'.[5] This aim can also be taken for granted. But it comes from the axiom that there are absolutes that are (relatively) clear for all to see. But this axiom needs to be sustained; and it has been sustained by the Christian faith.

The crisis in values we have been talking about—the moral bankruptcy—is a loss, surely, of this axiom, resulting from a loss of the Christian view about right and wrong. For nowadays in many quarters, it is felt that ethics, far from providing criteria for action, are there in the service of action. For example, some see modern social developments and scientific invention as autonomous. Thus devices of a most horrifying nature for the actual destruction of a large part of the planet—nuclear bombs—are produced. Ethicists are then predisposed to try to find justification for their continued existence and even their further development. At the other boundary of life—its construction rather than its destruction—ethicists are predisposed to try to find justification for alarming, if not horrific, experimentation on the human embryo as well as free-for-all abortion.

So ethics become exclusively inductive and *never* deductive. How can it be deductive, if there are no basic standards of right and wrong from which to deduce principles to apply? But unashamedly the Christian faith, as taught by Christ and his apostles, can have no truck with any such situationalism. Of course, there is a place for inductive reasoning. New developments occur in science; and so the church looks to see if there are justifications for seeing them as being right (if not, it must say they are wrong). This method has been used in the Protestant churches over contraception. But the arguments for its rightness are not based on instinct! Rather, they are based on given or absolute principles from the Bible that show how in marriage contraception is the way of responsibility. This is induction, but applying revealed truth to reach its conclusion.

Similarly there has to be a level of induction in the nuclear debate. There is no absolute principle that directly fits the problems. But that doesn't mean to say that absolute principles cannot *indirectly* apply. But with a loss of any view of absolutes, why should politicians bother with such principles? Naked politics is all that is left—*on both sides!*

Of course, none of these issues are clear-cut. But the absence of absolutes will most often lead to a defence of the status quo and the autonomy of the technician. This is pure barbarism. The fact that rockets, reactors, womb evacuators and test-tubes have taken the place of stones, wooden clubs and primitive child sacrifice is of minimal significance. Might is once again right. This is animal rather than human behaviour. Because some have ceased to believe in the Christian way, they have lost the middle axioms of moral absolutes and standards; and so they have lost the ability to say that anything is definitely right or wrong.

Law and human dignity

Of course, there is a legal spin-off from these particular moral aims and axioms. In the liberal West the idea was, as Demant summarizes it, 'To secure that the positive laws of particular states and legislatures were not treated as absolute and that they should be dependent on the constitution of reality—sometimes called Natural Law or Natural Rights.'[6]

This is very important. For it means that the law is above any ruler. The ruler is an instrument and not the source of the law. Thus you have a great safeguard. For this admits an appeal against the decision of the ruling authority. In fact this is the separation of the judiciary from the executive.

A third aim of Western liberalism is one we have already touched on—or we touched on its related axiom. It is the aim that all men deserve moral respect and legislative protection. So all are to be equal before the law. But this aim, as with other aims, must not be taken for granted. For it depends on an important axiom that is by no means inevitable. Indeed it depends on something like the Judaeo-Christian world view. For this is the axiom that suggests that a universal common characteristic belongs to all human beings. So all men and women are seen to be equal at a fundamental level. And that is why everyone deserves moral respect and legislative protection. The common factor, according to this liberal axiom, transcends all the differences of religion, nation, race, class or sex. It also lies behind all differences of position or rank and all differences of function in the social structure.

But, here if anywhere, we have faith-related aims and axioms. There is the need for the belief that man is made in the image of God; it is *this* that produces the common factor. It is obvious that the common factor does not, and cannot, have its roots in man's social relationships themselves; rather it must be related to a belief that is, so to speak, above these relationships. For the harsh realities of life would make us think that all men are *un*equal. Inequality is inherent in man by nature (some are born strong and some are born weak) and by function (some end up as bosses and some end up as bossed!). That is why, if man's significance is confined to the secular—to this world and to man's place or job in society—there can be no equality and no common element for the human condition, other than the accidents of birth. But this is no more than being animal. There will be nothing that is essentially *human*. 'It is by virtue of men standing in relation to a reality over and above their concrete place in social history, that men can speak of "our common humanity",' argues Demant.[7]

So here, then, are some of the key aims of what we know as Western liberal democracy. The majority in the United Kingdom still, I would submit, share these as aims. But the aims will not thrive or even survive unless backed up by axioms; and the axioms in turn need the Christian faith to back them up. It is without doubt that these axioms have sprung out of the Judaeo-Christian faith. They have then been crucial in forming the aims we all want in society. A plant severed from its root system will not survive for long since it is without nourishment; so it is with aims and axioms in the life of a culture. But things are changing.

There is now an awareness that all is not well. We have realized this for two decades. So there is some rethinking going on. In the Christian understanding 'repentance' is fundamentally 'rethinking'. That is the literal translation of the word the New Testament writers used for repentance. Interestingly, Gordon Ratray Taylor wrote a book entitled *Rethink*. In it he expressed the view that 'the Western World is engaged in a massive rethink which cannot fail to prove a turning point in its development'.[8]

The impact of technology, if nothing else, has forced on us some major rethinking about where we are going. For technology has shown itself to be a threat to many of these liberal human values, and it has highlighted their fragility. Far from bringing freedom, it has often brought a dehumanizing and alienating form of bondage! Jerome Weisner, a Provost of the Massachusetts Institute of Technology, put it forcefully like this:

> At the same time that technology emancipates man, freeing him from the necessity to slave at manual labour for a bare subsistance and promising him the opportunity for fulfilment as a truly human being, it threatens to dehumanize him more completely than the often uneven struggle of earlier times. This is why so many of our fellow citizens feel so cheated, so alienated.[9]

This dehumanizing doesn't have to be argued for. We see it in both the frustrations of suburbia and the deprivations of the inner city.

Priorities

We are back to the root problem of trying to meet spiritual or psychological needs by economic activity—the supply of goods. This is the failure to realize that man does not live by bread alone. And it is this that is the crisis facing governments of both the left and the right, although often they are unable to recognize it. In consequence the political debate is too often over which is the best method of producing these goods. But the real public debate needs to be much wider. It needs to be widened beyond the technical details of economics. For the background assumptions of a culture are all-important.

In the 1970s the Archbishop of Canterbury, Dr Coggan, saw this. He launched a 'Call to the Nation' for thought and prayer, on this basis: 'That there is a great body of seriously-minded men and women who are deeply concerned, *not only about the economy of our nation, but about its spiritual condition.*' This call was only partially responded to, partly because the Archbishop was ahead of his time in both the church and the nation; and partly because of problems of presentation. The then Bishop of Southwark contradicted the Archbishop by saying that the economy creates spirituality, and not vice-versa, as the Archbishop was suggesting. This further muddied the message. The Bishop of Southwark was in fact advocating the old Pelagian view that works come before belief (a view that the church rejected long ago).

Pelagian statements, of course, are useful as a corrective to remind us that belief must issue in works; and spirituality, if it is genuine, must work itself out in the transformation of society, and not just in 'super-spirituality'. But such statements must in no way mute the church's primary message about God, man, the world, sin, forgiveness in Jesus Christ, new life in the Holy Spirit and eternity.

That is perhaps why the nation, whether requested to by Archbishops or not, needs to address itself once again to such a call. It may have been premature on the part of Dr Coggan, but it was perfectly reasonable and vitally necessary. The time may now be ripe. For there are resources today that can help in analysis and rethinking. There are many younger and thoughtful Christians willing to assist the process. The evangelical renaissance referred to earlier means that there is taking place a recovery of biblical and apostolic Christianity that is politically and socially aware.

6

The Biblical Tradition

It was Hitler's notorious minister of propaganda, Goebbels, who said that 'churchmen dabbling in politics should take note that their only task is to prepare for the world hereafter'. We have already seen where this led the 'German Christians'—to a position of spiritual and political *laissez-faire*. But, as we have been arguing, the great need is for Christian people to engage in the public arena. The first need is to articulate in the Public Square Christian belief in its basic shape. Only then can axioms be maintained and aims supported.

But some may be asking, 'What is the Christian basis for thinking about politics and society? What is there in the Bible that can help us?' To answer those questions we need to look at the Old Testament, particularly prophecy (and its contrast with something similar, yet very different, from the period between Old and New Testament times—that is apocalyptic); we need also, of course, to look at the New Testament and the teaching of Jesus.

Prophecy

Prophecy is one of the key categories of the Bible. A prophet was a spokesman. In one passage of the Old Testament God is reported as saying to Moses, the Hebrew leader: 'See, I make you as God to Pharaoh; and Aaron your brother shall be your prophet' (Ex 7:1). Aaron was to be Moses' spokesman. Aaron's task was not to speak on his own behalf, but on Moses' behalf. So it was with the prophets of God. They were to speak on God's behalf.

Furthermore, their task was seen not so much in terms of 'futurology' as in terms of the communication of God's word about the *present*. True, the future was seen as important; but this was mainly because of its bearing on the present.

Prophecy in the Old Testament was, however, seen as something wider than the utterances of individual prophets. The Jews divided up the Old Testament into three sections: 'The Law and the Prophets and others that have followed in their steps,' to quote Ecclesiasticus.[1] The prophets referred to here were more than the books associated with individual prophets, such as Isaiah, Jeremiah and Ezekiel. The prophets of the Jewish tradition included the historical books of Joshua, Judges, Samuel and Kings. These were known as the 'former prophets'. What we today understand as the books of the prophets were known as the 'latter prophets'.

But this is of significance for the church's understanding of political and national events. For the events of public history, according to the former prophets, reveal God's will and purposes. For the ancient Jews understood that God acted in what we today would call public and political affairs, just as much as in the affairs of private, personal and religious life. So the prophetic task was to interpret these past events in terms of God's justice and mercy; and that interpretation was intended to suggest ways of repentance and reformation in the present. In this way the future would be a future of hope.

So the Bible sees the wider stage of history and public life as able to reveal God's will for man; and the prophets were God's spokesmen about what God was doing on that wider stage. They employed their words in various ways and styles, depending on each one's personality. But these words, nevertheless, were understood as also *coming from God*.

Much of what the prophets said was in relation to what God was doing in the public realm. And that is not surprising, because very little for the Jew was private. The personal, for example, was not considered private, in the sense of not being of interest to the community. That's why sexual morality was considered just as much a matter of public concern as cheating the poor. Immorality at the personal or communal level affected the totality of society. Both sorts of immorality were condemned by the prophets.

Jeremiah, for example, was a man who said in no uncertain terms that God was and would be judging the nation in the events of history. The people were rejecting God; the religious leaders were failing in their duty; false beliefs were being held; and the nation would suffer politically (actually, at the hands of the Babylonians). And you don't need a degree in theology to see the relevance of that for today!

Clearly the prophets related the public realm and the political world to God's purposes. So must we. And their constant theme was that the sin of disobedience led to judgement; and disobedience was first and foremost rejecting (or ignoring) the God of Abraham, Isaac and Jacob, the God who had brought liberation from oppression and slavery in Egypt, and who at Sinai had given the Law. The prophets saw this rejection as leading invariably, on the one hand, to sexual immorality and the breakdown of personal relationships; and, on the other hand, to social injustice and corruption, with the breakdown of social and communal relationships. The nation would thus be weakened; before long there would be national disintegration. Military defeat and surrender would lead to some people being transported to distant places; others would be refugees. And history has proved the prophets were right!

Apocalyptic

So the canonical or biblical prophets show that Goebbels was wrong, as have been all those who before and since have echoed his sentiments. But the significance of the biblical prophets is made clearer if we focus on a type of utterance that subtly contrasts with the prophets, namely apocalyptic.

Apocalyptic had similarities to prophecy, but it was really very different. It flourished a century or two before Christ— long after the great Hebrew prophets were dead; and its literature goes under some very exotic titles, such as *The Apocalypse of Enoch, The Assumption of Moses, The Testaments of the Twelve Patriarchs*—to name but three. But these and similar books were never included in the Bible.

The starting point for the apocalyptic philosophy is the problem of suffering—whether public or personal, whether due to sin or not. And this philosophy led to four important contrasts between the writers of apocalyptic and the prophets.

We will ignore the formal differences, such as the fact that the apocalyptic writers were very academic; their 'prophecies' were probably constructed in a library; they produced artificial dream scenarios; and they impersonated ancient biblical heroes. We must concern ourselves with their basic beliefs; for in them they expressed a world-view that was alternative to the prophetic world-view; and their philosophy of history was very different from that of biblical prophecy. Accordingly it was never accepted or endorsed by the Christian church.

So what then are the contrasts? There are four obvious ones.

First, the prophets referred to the past and the future because of their relevance to the present, as we have said; but the apocalyptists had little concern for the present. The present was evil and God would only act at the end of time. Of course, the prophets also had hope for the future but they saw God working in the present as well. The apocalyptist, however, saw God only as the God who *will* come. He is not the God who comes to his people *in history*. 'The apocalyptists do not view the coming of the Kingdom as the final act of God who is constantly acting in history,' wrote the biblical scholar, George Ladd.[2]

Secondly, there is pessimism in apocalyptic in quite a marked way. The blessings of the kingdom, it is felt, cannot be experienced in the present. This age has been abandoned to evil and suffering.

Thirdly, all is predetermined; why bother, then, with human initiative? One apocalyptic writer put the position like this: 'For he [God] has weighed the age in the balance, and measured the times by measure, and numbered the times by number; and he will not move nor arouse them until that measure is fulfilled.'[3] The prophets also knew God was sovereign; but, as Jonah learnt, they had to preach for repentance, as God was a God of mercy. So they looked for a present response from God.

The fourth contrast follows from this deterministic attitude. It is what has been called 'ethical passivity'. 'The apocalyptists,' says George Ladd, 'are not motivated by strong moral or evangelical urgency.' And he well sums up their position:

Apocalyptic eschatology [the study of the 'last things'] has lost the dynamic concept of God who is redemptively active in history. The apocalyptists, contrary to the prophets, despaired of history, feeling that it was completely dominated by evil. Hope was reposed only in the future. The harsh experiences of the last two centuries B.C. left the apocalyptists pessimistic of any divine visitation in history. God would visit his people to deliver them from evil only at the end of history . . . Redemptive history becomes altogether eschatology; and eschatology has become a guarantee of ultimate salvation, not an ethical message to bring God's people face to face with the will of God.[4]

So to recap: the biblical view of history is the prophetic philosophy of history. The apocalyptic view is rejected. This is why the church has to have *some* hope for the present and can't ignore the Public Square. It knows that the present is not necessarily 'the Day of the Lord' in all its completion. But in the present the church has to seek positively to help make God's world conform more to God's will.

Jesus and the kingdom

It was into a world with such contrasting views and beliefs that Jesus came 'preaching the gospel of God, and saying, "The time is fulfilled, and the kingdom of God is at hand; repent, and believe in the gospel"' (Mk 1:14-15). His message and the message of the New Testament generally was that in him God had *begun* his new work. In the incarnation and resurrection of Jesus the new age and the long-awaited 'Day' had begun to dawn.

But nevertheless the New Testament makes it clear that this dawning awaits a completion at the time when Jesus 'will come again to judge the living and the dead', as the Creed affirms. The present is, therefore, an age of ambiguity. It is, to use Paul's metaphor, the age of the 'first fruits'. The first fruits are more than mere blossom. They are the first ripe apples. But they are not the harvest.

The mistakes, therefore, can still be twofold. Either we can assume that God has done nothing and is doing nothing now in terms of establishing his kingdom of 'righteousness and peace and joy in the Holy Spirit' (Rom 14:17). The result of this is a modern form of 'apocalypticism', with a withdrawal from the world and the feeling that involvement will achieve nothing. So, it is felt, the church need not waste its time in the public arena.

Or, on the other hand, we can assume that the harvest has fully come. In the latter case institutions, from states to religious congregations, are structured on the assumption of the *present* perfectibility of mankind. The result is anything from oppressive theocracies or socialist tyrannies to perfectionist religious sects.

So, to use the categories of prophecy and apocalyptic, the New Testament teaching is prophetic in its approach to society, and it is realistic. Jesus taught that there will be 'wars and rumours of wars' in this present age. But he also taught, 'blessed are the peacemakers'. Good is possible, but not perfection. But that doesn't mean that an ideal of perfection should not help shape present policies. Indeed it must. But the consciousness that we can now only have approximations to that ideal helps us avoid all dangerous and frustrating utopianisms.

This tension of living in the overlap of two ages is expressed in the New Testament concept of citizenship. This is seen as twofold. On the one hand 'our citizenship [or, commonwealth] is in heaven,' as Paul taught. Yet he was fully aware that the people he taught that to could also be Roman citizens and citizens of Philippi (Phil 3:20). They were, as we are, both under God *and* under Caesar.

And there are three possibilities of handling this tension of living in two realms in the period 'between the times'.

First, we can be totally immersed in Caesar's secular world and its demands. At the political level that is the failure to witness to the religious dimension in public life. At the non-political personal level that means 'eat, drink and be merry' —the practice of hedonism. More respectably, we can be all absorbed with 'the cares of the world, and the delight in riches, and the desire for other things'; and Jesus said that if you want to 'throttle back' on God and his demands, this is the way to do it (Mk 4:19).

Secondly, we can withdraw and renounce the world. The 'pillar-saints' and the 'inclusi' were extreme examples of this approach. There was the famous Simon Stylites, for example. It is reported that

> he tried living in a cavern; he tried digging a grave and living in it with nothing but his head exposed. Finally, in AD 423, he built himself a pillar six feet high and began to live on the top of it. He never came down. For no less than thirty-seven years he lived on the top of his pillar, which was gradually heightened until it was sixty feet high.[5]

The inclusi were, literally, 'shut-ins'. They would find some corner in a monastery and get themselves bricked in with only a slit for the minimum of food to be passed to them. Apparently one person lived like this for twenty-five years. 'Are you alive?' someone asked through the narrow opening. 'I believe,' he answered, 'that I am dead to the world.'[6]

But, thirdly, we do not have either to be immersed in the world or to be isolated from it. We can be involved, but with a detachment from all that is evil. Jesus' prayer for his disciples was just this: 'I do not pray that thou shouldest take them out of the world, but that thou shouldest keep them from the evil one' (Jn 17:15). Indeed, he then said in his prayer, 'As thou didst send me into the world, so I have sent them into the world' (17:18).

Political involvements

The presumption therefore seems to be that we should aim to be 'good citizens'. The New Testament indicates that this involves public responsibility at the financial level. We are to pay 'dues, taxes and revenue', as stated in chapter 13 of

Paul's epistle to the Romans. That is a chapter which has been foundational for Christian political thinking down the centuries. It begins like this:

> Let every person be subject to the governing authorities. For there is no authority except from God, and those that exist have been instituted by God. Therefore he who resists the authorities resists what God has appointed, and those who resist will incur judgement.

Whatever other message might be conveyed by that, the idea that social order and stability is a good thing comes across. And order and stability are good. It has been part of the Christian tradition that bad government is better than no government. Sometimes it is hard to believe that, but we should ask those who have experienced anarchy. However, as we shall see, that doesn't necessarily mean we have to acquiesce under *all* governments, however intolerable.

This passage in Romans also teaches that God himself is the source of all authority (and that includes political authority). It tells us that those who exercise authority on earth do so by delegation from God. They may not acknowledge this, but it is nevertheless so. Therefore, to disobey them is to disobey God. These authorities—the people who exercise authority—are to be seen as servants of God.

Looking at some examples of political leadership, we may find that hard to believe. But we must remember that Paul was writing under the emperorship of Nero! Paul was not naive but neither was he sentimental. He was able to analyse objectively. Ideally, the individual intention of a political leader and the divine intention should coincide. But Paul knew they often didn't. They certainly didn't in the case of Nero. But in so far as Nero embodied the duty of government to bring relative order through various sanctions, this could be seen as God's will. Nero was therefore fulfilling a function that was God-given.

But what if a civil authority exceeds its God-given function? Is this teaching of Paul *carte blanche* for governments to do what they like? What if Caesar demands more than Caesar's share? Jesus, who had defined the political and religious spheres, had said: 'Render to Caesar the things that are Caesar's, and to God the things that are God's' (Mk 12:17). But what if Caesar demands God's share? What if Caesar forbids what God orders, or orders what God forbids?

Compromise

In answering that question we have to avoid an unbiblical rigorism. The state can never legislate for perfection. Much will be happening in the world that is morally wrong or questionable. But not every issue can be fought. In the world the New Testament advocates a level of compromise and an absence of rigorism over unimportant matters.

An example of this is when Paul tells the Corinthian Christians that when they go to a dinner party they shouldn't ask too many questions about where the meat has come from. They might find out that it had been part of an idolatrous sacrifice. There is a place in social life for the 'blind eye'.

Now compromise must never be deception. That is a wrong and cowardly approach. Rather, what we are talking about is a realization that some things are of secondary importance; and living 'between the times', there will always be loose ends.

Jesus gives us an example of one instance of compromise with the world around. It was in his answer to the Pharisees when he spoke about God and Caesar. The context of that remark was this. The Roman authorities annually levied a poll tax on every Jewish adult male. But this tax was deeply resented by most Jews. On the one hand it was a sign of national subjection; on the other hand it had to be paid in silver coinage, stamped with the Emperor's laurelled head. And this violated the strict interpretation of the Jewish law against 'images'.

On this occasion Jesus had been asked a difficult question (from a political point of view): 'Is it lawful to pay taxes to Caesar, or not?' It was a trick question. His answer was simply this: 'Show me a coin.' And someone did. But that immediately gave the game away. The Pharisees, who were trying to trick Jesus into formally denying either God or Caesar, had their hypocrisy exposed. For in their pockets they *already had* Roman coins, whatever were their scruples. So George Caird comments: 'By accepting the Roman coinage and with it the benefits conferred by Rome in the way of economic stability and political order [Jesus' interrogators] had committed themselves to an answer to their own question.'[7]

Jesus was in fact saying that there may be things you dislike or disagree with in the state, but as you receive its benefits you have a responsibility for involvement in it, even where it is compromised. So 'render to Caesar the things that are Caesar's, and to God the things that are God's'.

Disobedience

But while some are *never* willing to compromise, some *always* compromise. Both are inevitably wrong responses. The latter is wrong because sometimes, like Luther, we have to say: 'Here I stand.' Not all issues are secondary. Sometimes in public life the state (or any other form of organized community) has demanded God's share at a fundamental level. Christians down the centuries have experienced this, and in some parts of the world still experience it.

In cases like that the Christian response has been that of Peter. When the Jewish High Priest and the Council forbade him and the other early Christians to preach and teach about

Jesus, Peter, along with the other apostles, simply said words of protest that have been an inspiration to many down the centuries: 'We must obey God rather than men' (Acts 5:29).

The state can go terrifyingly wrong, as we have experienced more than once this present century. When the state tries to encompass the whole of life, we call it totalitarian. It is a likely consequence of the retreat of religion and God from the Public Square or public consciousness. The state, as it embraces more and more, may have the most benign of intentions, but it must never play God!

In the New Testament there are two sides to the state. In Romans chapter 13 there is Paul's ruler who is a 'servant of God'. But in the vision in the book of Revelation you have the 'beast rising out of the sea' that receives authority from the great dragon (Rev 13:1). This authority it uses to enforce universal worship of itself and to exterminate all those that refuse to worship it. Here is a picture of the sort of state Rome was becoming. It was abusing its God-given function.

Another image for the state comes later in the book of Revelation, where there is a reference to the great harlot, 'Babylon the great, mother of harlots and of earth's abominations . . . drunk with the blood of the saints and the blood of the martyrs of Jesus' (17:5-6). And Babylon was the code name for Rome!

Rome brought order, justice and peace in the *Pax Romana*. But gradually, for political advantage, the Emperor demanded that he be worshipped. At first the Emperors were no doubt embarrassed by the Emperor cult. But bit by bit the Roman state began to see a far-reaching use for it in unifying the Empire. So there was a requirement that once a year citizens should burn a pinch of incense to Caesar and say, 'Caesar is Lord.' But Christians refused. They had to disobey; they had to obey God rather than man. They could only say, 'Jesus is Lord.'

7
Secularism and Liberalism

Much water has flowed under the bridge since Jesus spoke about God and Caesar. First there was all the period up to Constantine's Edict of Toleration in AD 313.

The early church

The church of those early days formed what Bishop Gore called 'a sort of spiritual aristocracy'.[1] But there was no way the church could involve itself in government or take a major initiative in political life. It was the church of the catacombs.

This was the age of persecution, and the blood of the martyrs was the seed of the church. It was the age when the church was very much set over against society. It maintained a high level of discipline. You didn't become a Christian unless you chose to, for it was still dangerous to be a believer. And certainly at this time no one was *compelled* to be a Christian. 'Religion is not to compel religion,' said Tertullian.[2]

The church, not having to be God's servant for justice and so not having to wield the sword, was predominantly pacifist.

For Athanasius the great mark of Christianity was that it turned swords into ploughshares.[3] Gore comments:

> It is from this period of the Church's life, already past, that Augustine, seventy years after Constantine's Edict of Toleration, draws his picture of the City of God—a city without earthly frontiers, without distinctions of nationality or secular status, of civilization or barbarism; a city which comprises the dead no less than the living; a city whose citizenship depends upon participation in a common faith, obedience to common laws, inspiration by a common Spirit—a heavenly *civitas,* set up in the midst of the earthly, yet for ever distinct from it, and founded upon a contrary principle.[4]

But then came the day when the Emperor himself acknowledged the Christian God as the true God. And the church, some would say, lost its innocence. It became at home in the corridors of power and eventually tried to organize a united Christendom. The idea was to identify the universal Empire with the universal church. In the process the principle of the essential 'voluntariness' in matters of belief was forgotten, as were the tight entry requirements for membership of the church. But for all its faults these 'middle ages' tried to bring the whole of life under the sovereignty of Christ.

Then came the Renaissance and the Reformation; the result was that the existing relationships between the church and the state were often challenged and changed. And none was to challenge the fundamental assumptions of politics and religion more than Machiavelli (1469-1527).

This Renaissance political philosopher from Florence is a byword for ruthless cunning. But his main importance is that he was among the first in the new age to separate politics from the Christian religion and morality. For him all that mattered was power (this was needed to keep order). It didn't matter how you got it. All are motivated by greed and fear, he said. Others will break their promises, so we can break ours. His book *The Prince* was condemned by the church, but its principles were reflected in the regimes of the new rulers of Europe, especially in that of Cesare Borgia. Here indeed was the beginning of secularism, and Machiavelli was one of its founding fathers.

The beginnings of secularism

Something sinister was happening in this break of the link between politics and the Christian religion. For the link is essential as a means of preventing the state from being absolute or ultimate. This is because in the Christian faith God alone is absolute. So whatever relation the state may have to its own subjects, it is certainly subordinate to God. Indeed, in the middle ages the sovereign was seen as holding a divine commission, but not to do whatever he liked. He was to uphold God's law. This led to the doctrine of 'divine right'. That meant that people had to obey the king. To disobey was sin. But this was only so long as the king maintained God's justice. If he became a tyrant he was to be deposed. Thomas Aquinas was quite definite:

> 'A tyrannical government is not "just" since it is directed, not to the common good, but to the private good of the ruler,' as the philosopher [Aristotle] states. So there is no sedition in disturbing a government of this kind, unless indeed the tyrant's rule be disturbed so inordinately that his subjects suffer greater harm from the consequent disturbance than from the tyrant's government. Indeed it is the tyrant rather that is guilty of sedition, since he encourages discord and sedition among his subjects, that he may lord over them more securely; for this is tyranny, being conducive to the private good of the ruler and to the injury of the multitude.[5]

If Machiavelli was one of secularism's founding fathers, a second was the Englishman, Thomas Hobbes (1588-1679). He was secular in that he excluded God from his political theory. Working from the assumption that everyone is essentially selfish, he argued that government comes about by everyone giving up their independence and submitting to one man or assembly of men. This produces human society, he argued. For the natural state of man is that 'every man is enemy to every man', and 'the life of man [is] solitary, poor, nasty, brutish and short'.[6] So human society comes from surrendering individual rights in a 'commonwealth'. But the sovereign then has absolute rights over everything, the church and the individual conscience included!

Of course, this is pure mythology, as with all social contract theories. The 'power' of the story depends on whether you like the end result. The House of Commons in 1666 clearly didn't like the end result, for it censured *Leviathan,* the book in which Hobbes argued his position, and Hobbes was forbidden to publish any more in England. But how dangerous was Hobbes?

Behind all the fanciful arguing, there was a dangerous proposition. It was this: that the origin of government (the rule of the one man or assembly) is the origin of society. The state and society are coterminous. But the Christian division of the things that belong to God and the things that belong to Caesar makes it clear that Caesar (or the state) doesn't own the whole of society. The life of man can't all be subsumed by politics or be included in the sphere of government. Of course, to identify the state or government with society is to say that to overthrow an existing government is to dissolve society! A very convenient doctrine for unjust rulers.

Modern secularism

Some, of course, put all the blame for modern secularism on the Reformers! The Reformers, they say, saw the whole of life as a 'calling'; thus everything was sacred. The secular was baptized. The trouble then, so it is argued, is that before long the technically sacred—the life of prayer, Bible reading, worship and contemplation—gets squeezed out and ignored. What you are left with is worldliness, by whatever name you call it. There is no doubt some truth in this. But this can only be one of the strands in the evolution of secular attitudes.

Another strand has been the huge problems that have arisen for the church from new social developments. The church has not always known how to begin to tackle them and perhaps has too easily drifted with the secular world. Troeltsch well summed up the social problem of the modern world as 'vast and complicated'. It includes 'the problem of the capitalist economic period and of the industrial proletariat created by it; and of the growth of militaristic and bureaucratic giant states; of the enormous increase in population, which affects colonial and world policy; of the mechanical technique, which produces enormous masses of material and links up and mobilizes the whole world for the purposes of trade, but which also treats men and labour like machines'.[7] But whatever the precise cause of modern secularism, for our present purposes Christopher Dawson seems near the mark:

> Our civilization has become secularized largely because the Christian element has adopted a passive attitude and allowed the leadership of culture to pass to the non-Christian minority. And this cultural passivity has not been due to any profound existentialist concern with the human predicament and divine judgement, but on the contrary to a tendency toward social conformity and too ready an acceptance of the values of secularized society. It is the intellectual and social inertia of Christians that is the real obstacle to a restoration of Christian culture.[8]

But we will not fully understand modern secularism in the Western liberal tradition unless we understand something of the earlier discussions on liberty. John Locke (1631-1704) in one sense started the modern discussion on liberty because of his desire for religious freedom and toleration. He was a religious man himself, but he had experienced too much intolerance in his younger days. So he argued for the freedom to worship God as a man's conscience dictated. This was the supreme, essential, freedom. He argued for this as a natural right and not just as a piece of social convenience. It wasn't just that there would be a more settled society with religious tolerance. Rather, each man and woman had a right not to be interfered with as far as their religious faith was concerned. Of course, once that right was established there were other rights and freedoms. There was, for example, the freedom to meet with like-minded people and to express opinions.

But the great spokesman for liberty, and a secularist at the same time, was a man we have already mentioned, John Stuart Mill (1806-1873). His essay *On Liberty* has been called 'the first modern exposition of a theory of the secular state'. Mill's view in short was this:

> The only purpose for which power can be rightfully exercised over any member of a civilized community against his will, is to prevent harm to others. His own good, either physical or moral, is not a sufficient warrant. He cannot rightfully be compelled to do or forbear because it will be better for him to do so, because it will make him happier, because in the opinions of others, to do so would be wise, or even right.[9]

Mill thus believed that law was a restriction on liberty; it should only be imposed to secure the wider interests of liberty itself. He agreed that liberty has to be curtailed in some respects, otherwise there is no liberty at all. My liberty to go safely about my normal business is secured by legally restricting the liberty of anyone who wants to shoot me!

Limitations of liberalism

Of course, there was truth in what Mill said. But the problem with his view was threefold. First, it was too narrow. It was pointed out by T. H. Green (1836-1882) and others that there is a wider view. It is not only liberty that can be seen to be positive, but law as well:

> It [law] is not only a means by which I restrain the liberty of others to injure me; still more fundamentally it is the means by which I secure my own liberty to live as a good citizen against my own occasional desires to act otherwise. The law that forbids murder is not the expression of determination in one set of people to hang another set of people if they commit this crime; it expresses the determination of each of us to impose restraint upon himself if ever he feels murderous; and to that end to vote the death penalty (or whatever it may be) to himself if he yields to such an impulse.[10]

Secondly, Mill was unrealistic. No man is an island. Therefore, by causal connections it can be argued that harm done by an individual to himself ultimately harms another. At the most obvious level, if his excessive smoking causes lung cancer, *that* is a drain on the taxpayer in medical costs. If his drinking causes alcoholism, *that* harms his wife and children. If his sexual immorality gives him AIDS, *that* will be a problem for others. And it can be argued that omitting to reach one's true potential in anything is robbing others of one's usefulness.

Thirdly, Mill's long-term effect was to destroy a 'consensus' of shared values in society. That probably was not his intention. His main concern was to stop majority governments *enforcing* consensus:

> Let us suppose, therefore, that the government is entirely at one with the people, and never thinks of exerting any power of coercion unless in agreement with what it conceives to be their voice. But I deny the right of the people to exercise such coercion, either by themselves or by their government.[11]

But the result over the last 100 years has been this: when there is a minority opinion it is not simply that the majority has been prevented from enforcing its views on the minority. The majority is often prevented from expressing its views *at all,* even in the interests of peaceful persuasion.

Mill himself was only trying to protect, for example, atheists from the charge of blasphemy in the courts and to secure freedom of belief (or unbelief). But the long-term result of this libertarianism has been that today the majority in society (Christian adherents with various levels of commitment) are often deprived of *their* freedom of expression. This is particularly the case with regard to the electronic media—that is, broadcasting.

Even when there is no legal restriction there is often a psychological restriction on articulating clearly a Christian majority position. Social custom has elevated the concept of reticence over disagreements, so as to avoid giving offence to minorities who disagree with majority opinion. This situation, to be fair to Mill, was not something he would have wanted or promoted. For he was concerned to *express,* not suppress opinions. His concern was to give the minority view a fair hearing. Logical criticism was good, he felt, for everyone: 'He who knows only his own side of the case knows little of that.' But obviously the majority must also have a fair hearing.

Religious freedom

The notion of tolerance for varying religious beliefs—one of the humane fruits of the Enlightenment—has had an odd twist. It started life as the freedom to practice your own religion in whatever way you chose. So in England it meant that dissenters and Roman Catholics were free to dissent or give allegience to the Pope. It also meant the freedom to believe there was no God.

But religious freedom was never meant to be the freedom *from* religion. Yet in the interests of a so-called neutrality, that is what is in danger of coming about today. For this sort of freedom is sometimes now being enforced upon people. Thus in schools headmasters backpeddle or even refuse to have Christian worship regularly, and religious instruction is a Cinderella by comparison with other subjects.

So we have got to the odd position of making religious freedom the opposite of religious observance. This it was never meant to be. Thus an obsession with neutrality ends up with not neutrality but, on the one hand, hostility to the Christian religion and on the other hand, what has been called 'the establishment of a religion of secularism'.

The idea of religious freedom was originally motivated by the desire to ensure a haven from religious tyranny. But it ends up tyrannizing religion! It pretends to be open and pluralistic. But pluralism, it has been well said, is a jealous God. 'When pluralism is established as dogma, there is no room for other dogmas. The assertion of other points of reference in moral discourse becomes, by definition, a violation of pluralism.'[12]

But things are changing. Political theorists, social scientists and sociologists generally have less confidence in secularist answers or secularist goals for society than in the days of Machiavelli, Hobbes, Locke and Mill.

But what really is secularism? The answer we give as to whether society today is secular depends on what our answer to this question is.

David Lyon, following Larry Shiner in 'The concept of secularization in empirical research', argues that we can mean five things by secularization.[13] First, there is 'the decline of religion'. This is when as a simple matter of fact religious beliefs and institutions lose their prestige. But as we have seen, it depends from which point of view you are looking at these beliefs and institutions—from an individual, congregational, denominational or national point of view.

Secondly, there is 'conformity with this world'. People

cease to be interested in the supernatural; and the problems of the present are all-absorbing. But here you have to distinguish between the interest of the various elites and the majority of the people. A few opinion formers may have a *recherché* interest in reading about the secularized Bloomsbury Set of the pre-war years in the Sunday supplements. Most people, one suspects, find their fads, habits and tastes of little interest.

Disengagement, transposition and desacralization

Thirdly, there is the 'disengagement of society from religion'. Religion therefore becomes 'privatized' and has less and less of a place in the Public Square—for example, in politics and education. But as we have seen, while this is undoubtedly possible and often happens, this is not necessarily what most people want. It may simply be due to certain unrecognized pressures or twists of circumstance.

Fourthly, there is 'the transposition of religious belief and institutions'. Marx provides a good example of this. For instead of 'the End' being the Second Coming of Jesus Christ, 'the End' becomes the ultimate, classless society after the economic revolution. We have seen too many transpositions of the doctrine of salvation, which for the Christian is through the forgiveness of sins and peace with God. In Herbert Spencer's version of evolutionary progressivism in the last century 'salvation' came via the process of time—'the better is the more evolved'. Freud this century saw 'salvation' virtually in terms of the fulfilment of our desires for sex, nutrition and power. But none of these transpositions has survived the test of time.

Fifthly, there is 'the desacralization of the world' (leaving nothing sacred). Modern science creates a 'disenchantment' and an increasing loss of the sense of the sacred. But as David Lyon has pointed out, desacralization can be a mark of a culture strong in religion. 'Was it not,' he asks, 'the very desacralizing tendencies within Protestantism (in asserting that nature is not itself infused with magic or mystery) which helped foster the early development of modern science?'[14]

But when the defining is done we still come back to the possibility that the anthropologist Emile Durkheim was right. He claimed that in all societies there has to be some sort of religion. None are ever completely secular. The word 'religion', of course, literally means 'binding' (Latin *religare*, 'to bind'). For it is religion that is the social 'glue'. Without it a society falls apart. There has to be some transcendent value or meaning that gives purpose to communal life and gives sanction to laws and rules. That is why the contest today is not between religion and irreligion; nor is the fundamental issue for society the question of whether it will be religious or secular. The question is, 'What religion is our society going to allow to shape its culture?' In the United Kingdom the alternatives are clear—is it going to be the religion of persuasive and tolerant Christianity, or the religion of aggressive and intolerant liberal humanism?

The decision will depend in part on how seriously Christian people over the next few years play their part in the public sphere. If they leave it exclusively to others, they will have only themselves to blame.

8

William Temple

One of the great figures in Christian social and political ethics this century was Archbishop William Temple (1881-1944). It may be true, as Edward Norman says, that his 'social thinking was in fact rather unoriginal'.[1] But his gift was to take other people's ideas and present them forcefully, clearly and with enthusiasm. A man with left-wing sympathies himself, he nevertheless knew that the church must not take part in party politics. He never wavered from his early conviction of 1912:

> The Church and the official representatives of the Church must keep themselves free from the entanglements of party politics. Their business is something far more fundamental and important; it is the formation of that mind and temper in the whole community which will lead to wholesome legislation by any party and all parties.[2]

So how precisely did Temple see political involvement?

First, he saw the state as having a *limited* public function that needed to be kept that way, and as being the one institution that was properly entitled to use force. So he established three fundamentals about the state:

> One, society is more than the State, and has a life which is largely independent of the State; two, social progress largely consists of the expression and development of that independence; three, the State is distinguished from other 'social cohesions' by the fact that it alone is entitled to use force in order to secure obedience to its command.[3]

Temple, therefore, endorsed the view that the Public Square was not to be identified with Parliament Square! He also knew that the greatest influence on the world by the church was not in political or social church pronouncements (or even fights with the Government!) but in the faithful 'daily round and common task' of individual believers in the world. 'Nine-tenths of the work of the Church in the world,' he said, 'is done by Christian people fulfilling responsibilities and performing tasks which in themselves are not part of the official system of the church at all.'[4]

He specifically referred to the work of evangelicals in the last century. He cited Wilberforce and his friends, who were involved in the abolition of the slave trade. But he recognized that there are other more humble people who act as the 'salt of the earth'. So he agreed 'that the task of the Church in the face of social problems is to make good Christian men and women. That is by far its most important contribution.'[5] However, in a democratic society each person has a responsibility as a citizen to exercise political influence. Each person is one of the 'powers that be' and so is responsible for justice and order. Most people, of course, don't want to be involved in politics as such. They haven't the time, energy or skill to play a useful part in active politics. But most people can identify the key issues from programmes like BBC Radio 4's *Today* or ITV's *News at Ten*. They can form some judgement about the central political figures and some of their public policies. Every five years they can register support or protest by a cross on a voting paper. Some can do more. But even that five-yearly vote has enormous influence. Politicians are always concerned with how the voters are going to respond. As we saw in the case of Sunday trading, they will now have to take account of the new *Christian* vote. Already this is the case in the United States. It is now becoming the case in the United Kingdom.

Engagement in politics

Temple argued that four factors should cause the church to engage in political affairs (in a non-party way). First, there are the claims of Christ-like love for those who suffer. Secondly, there is the fact that a social or economic system— whether it be socialist or capitalist—gives rise to certain values. Thirdly, there is the need for justice, as the Old Testament so clearly shows. Fourthly, there are the claims of the created order that God intended for man. God, indeed, has created man a social being.

But *how* should the church practically engage in politics? Temple reckoned there were three ways. One, its members should live positively for Jesus Christ in daily life, as has already been said; two, its members should vote responsibly every five years to promote Christian values (and in addition some should be actively involved in the political parties); but, three, the church itself—its clergy and teachers—needs to provide Christian men and women 'with a systematic statement of principles to aid them in doing these two things, and this will carry with it a denunciation of customs or institutions in contemporary life and practice which offend against those principles'.[6]

Naturally, up to this point he carried with him all those who wanted to oppose existing Government policies. He also carried the more 'revolutionary' elements who wanted to change the whole social order. For he was saying that the church needed to point out where the existing social and political order was in conflict with Christian principles.

But he immediately lost this support once he was heard to say that the church was *not* to dictate a solution or *means* for solving political problems. For he believed that the role of the church in social and political affairs was limited. It was limited, first, to teaching about *ends* and, secondly, to a criticism of existing means—those that did not achieve the prescribed ends or those that were self-evidently evil.

The Archbishop gave what has now become a famous analogy to illustrate his point:

> If a bridge is to be built, the Church may remind the engineer that it is his obligation to provide a really safe bridge; but it is not entitled to tell him whether, in fact, his design meets this requirement . . . in just the same way the Church may tell the politician what ends the social order should promote; but it must leave to the politician the devising of the precise means to those ends.[7]

The three ends that Temple advocated were fundamentally biblical: 'Freedom, fellowship, and service—these are the three principles of a Christian social order, derived from the still more fundamental Christian postulates that Man is a child of God and is destined for a life of eternal fellowship with Him.'[8]

So first, Temple was concerned that the social order should reflect the widest possible opportunities for personal responsibility and freedom. That is why he supported democracy as a form of government—it provides a chance for each person, even if only indirectly, to be involved and exercising a small measure of responsibility.

But Temple wanted freedom and responsibility to be positive—not just 'freedom from', but 'freedom for' creative and selfless living. Responsibility was not just for the sake of having a say, but for the sake of contributing to the common good.

Fellowship and service

Secondly, Temple saw social fellowship as an important end that needs to be put on to the public agenda. This is because much political theory focuses exclusively on the individual, on the one hand, and on the state on the other hand. So the debates focus around freedom, liberty and human rights, as individual concerns; and around peace, justice and the economy, as state concerns.

But the social order is not just made up of individuals and the state. For there are 'mediating' communities; paramount among these is the family. So no political theory is adequate that fails to do justice to the family. It is, in fact, in the mediating communities—the buffer groups between the individual and the state—that liberty is experienced.

But the family, although important, is not the only such community. There are also schools, colleges, trades unions, professional associations, cities, counties, the four nations in the United Kingdom, and of course, the church. It is a fact that revolutionary politics either ignores or tries to destroy these subordinate groups. They are too untidy. But the health of a society is intimately linked with its mediating structures. So obviously a key means of weakening, if not destroying, the whole social fabric is to attack these structures. That is why in the United Kingdom, questions that relate to the health of the family must be high on *party* political agendas (as on any other agendas)—that is, if we want to discover a new sense of social coherence and purpose. It is, after all, in families that cultural and religious values are transmitted most effectively.

Thirdly, Temple stressed service as an end in the social order. From a Christian point of view, he said, this begins with fulfilling one's calling.

The concept of calling or vocation is fundamental in Christian thinking. Max Weber argued, rather fancifully as many now think, that the Protestant doctrine of the calling was responsible for capitalism! But William Temple, nothing daunted, saw the neglect of a sense of calling as seriously wrong. 'Some young people,' he said, 'have the opportunity to choose the kind of work by which they will earn their living. To make that choice on selfish grounds is probably the greatest single sin that any young person can commit, for it is the deliberate withdrawal from allegiance to God of the greatest part of one's time and strength.'[9] Of course, he knew that many had no choice. In a time of unemployment many would be without work. But he believed circumstances (sometimes without choice) can be a means through which God's call comes to a man or woman. 'And his call is sometimes to self-sacrifice as well as to self-fulfilment . . . It is possible to accept the one job available, however distasteful and dreary, as God's call to me; and then I shall enter on it in the spirit of service.'[10]

But nevertheless, he recognized an obligation on society as a whole to try to make opportunities for vocation. To do this there has to be an acknowledgement that God is creative. So work should, in a measure, reflect his creative working. Therefore, men and women should not just be offered work opportunities that 'only a miracle of grace' could transform into self-evident vocations! However, even when work is dreary, it can and should be done as 'unto the Lord', and so also should more interesting work.

Rights and duties

Service, however, does not only imply calling or vocation. It will mean an emphasis on duties rather than rights. In the history of political ideas it is unfortunate that the French writer Rousseau (1712-1778) should have been the dominating influence in the French Revolution at the end of the eighteenth century; and it is unfortunate that Marx (1818-

1883) should have been the dominating influence in the economic revolution that began in the nineteenth century and has spread world-wide. For they, argued Temple, 'taught the democratic movement to take its stand on rights'.[11]

But there is only one safe way to true social progress. And that is not to be found in rights but in duties. In terms of social legislation and opportunities there may be no observable difference in a system that majors on rights from a system that majors on duties. Duties are the other side of the coin to rights. So what is a duty for one man—for example, that he observes a no-parking sign—is another man's right, that his drive-way is not obstructed. 'But the difference in the temper of the movement that rests on rights will be aggressive, violent, contentious; and the temper of a movement that rests on duties will be persuasive, public spirited, harmonious.'[12]

So Temple stressed three ends for society: freedom, fellowship and service. Having established these ends, he tried to apply them to particular instances. Because of his experience in the thirties he had a concern, as we have today, for unemployment. But his method prevented him from producing a *Christian* solution to unemployment. 'There neither is nor could be such a thing. Christian faith does not by itself enable its adherents to foresee how a vast multitude of people, each one partly selfish and partly generous, and an intricate economic mechanism will in fact be affected by a particular economic or political innovation.' But this didn't mean that he couldn't speak out strongly about the failure of society, and by implication, politicians: 'I cannot tell you what is the remedy; but I can tell you that a society of which unemployment . . . is a chronic feature, is a diseased society, and that if you are not doing all you can to find and administer the remedy, you are guilty before God.'[13]

The Archbishop knew that if the church followed his advice it would be attacked on two fronts: 'It will be told that is has become political when in fact it has been careful only to state principles and point to breaches of them; and it will be told by advocates of particular policies that it is futile because it does not support these.'[14]

Now, of course, churchmen may be right when they advocate specific political and economic remedies. But if so, Temple would say, it is probably like a theologian also being a competent engineer and making right judgements about bridge design. Such a man ought to be listened to, 'but this is altogether because he is a competent engineer . . . his theological equipment has nothing whatever to do with it.'[15]

So William Temple would have argued that it is because the church should only be concerned with ends and not means that it is possible for Christian people to come down on different sides of the political divide.

The middle way

The kingdom of God has been inaugurated in Jesus Christ with his life, death and resurrection, but it is not finally established—for that we await his return. Because that is so, we live with a level of ambiguity. There are possibilities of good now, but not of perfection. The danger is twofold. People may assume that no good at all can be achieved in the present and that everything has to await God's purposes at the last day. This was, we remember, the position of the apocalyptists in biblical times. A second danger is to assume that God's purposes can be achieved in the present if only we work hard enough or bring in the revolution. This was the position of various nationalist or Zealot-type movements in biblical times. Hopeless pessimism is a temptation that comes to some; revolutionary enthusiasm is a temptation that comes to others.

William Temple went for the middle way of 'realism'. But because he did not go in for revolutionary enthusiasm he has never been in favour with left-wing utopians. Nor is he in favour with some of them today!

Charles Elliott, who headed the British Council of Churches' Christian Aid for a period, has criticized 'the Temple method'. He calls it, 'So earthy, so empirical, so pragmatic.'[16] Elliott argues for a Christian utopianism. As with those who advocate Liberation Theology, one of his inspirations is the German theologian Jurgen Moltmann and his 'theology of hope': 'The key element of the theology of hope,' Elliott says, 'is the insistence that the present does not define the possibilities of the future.' Future dreams can come true.

Rather than being utopian he calls this 'visionary': 'The crucial difference between vision and utopia is less the content than the value we put upon it. We make visions into utopias when we are not prepared to die for them.' This is fighting talk. It is the mood of the political revolutionary. The sort of 'visions' that Elliott seems to have in mind are 'the end of racial exploitation in South Africa', 'the end of the fixation with class snobbery in the UK', 'a world in which no man luxuriates in excess and each man has enough'. All these every Christian would agree to. The disagreement is over method, attitude and expectation.

Temple taught the pathway of pragmatism. Elliott thinks this is not enough. Temple said that given the ends, we have to find the best way of reaching those ends; but this is not a distinctly church job. No, says Elliott—you can't just let the world choose the means. For means are not value-free.

Elliott cites a wage-dispute where there often would have to be a trade-off between equality and efficiency in settling it. 'At what point is it "right" to forego equality in order to increase efficiency?' asks Elliott. 'Different economists will solve that problem in different ways according to their own value systems.'

But, to argue on Temple's behalf, while this is undoubtedly true in some cases, it is clearly not true in all cases. And when it is true, the church's role is to ask questions and when necessary challenge policies. Temple did that when he challenged the economic means that led to unemployment; and on such occasions the church, or Christian people, must say to politicians, businessmen, managers or other professionals: 'Find another and better solution.'

But take the case in point—the pay dispute. In times of economic depression 'practical economics' are clearer cut and involve fewer value judgements; it is a question of efficiency or bankruptcy. The problem is greater in times of economic growth. Then the issue *does* depend on values. When a ship-yard is prospering, for example, and there is a reasonable level of efficiency, some will decide for higher pay over greater efficiency. True, in time market forces will bring a day of reckoning in some shape or form. But the economic 'value judgement' comes over whether you will have pleasure today and pain tomorrow; or a bit of pleasure today and only a bit of pain tomorrow; or pain today and pleasure tomorrow. Pragmatists like Temple would argue that sometimes you have to let non-Christians make these choices. We can't get out of the world, and there aren't enough Christians to go round to do everything. But we can be vigilant. Through the electoral process at various intervals we can express our views as to whether the right value judgements are being made or not.

Realism

So William Temple was a realist. That is the great contrast between William Temple and many of the liberal churchmen, of various shades, who today get involved in social affairs. This is seen nowhere more clearly than in his view of original sin. He knew, as Jesus taught, that ultimately sin proceeds out of the human heart. Of course, there is a reciprocal process with the structures of society when they are evil. These structures will reinforce sin. But Temple knew that a Christian social doctrine that ignores original sin isn't worth the paper it's written on.

It is because of original sin that we must not draw up a perfect social order and then tell people to establish it. This is the fault with Marxists and other liberationists. But as Temple pointed out, an ideal or perfect social order is hard to define. Does it mean the social order that is fitted for perfect men and women? If so, it would be disastrous, as it would be wrecked 'in a fortnight'. Or does it mean the social order that is ideal and perfectly fitted for men and women in all their weakness and sinfulness? 'If it is the latter, there is no reason for expecting the church to know what it is.'[17] So we have to take original sin seriously.

Original sin has had a bad press. Temple defined it like this:

> I am the centre of the world I see; where the horizon is depends on where I stand . . . But I am not the centre of the world, or the standard of reference as between good and bad; I am not, and God is. In other words, from the beginning I put myself in God's place. This is my original sin . . . Education may make my self-centredness less disastrous by widening my horizon of interest; so far it is like the climbing of a tower, which widens the horizon for physical vision while leaving me still the centre and standard of reference . . . complete deliverance can be effected only by the winning of my whole heart's devotion, the total allegiance of my will—and this only the Divine Love disclosed by Christ in His life and Death can do.[18]

Original sin does not mean that everything a man or woman does is inherently evil. But it does mean that everything is infected with this problem: that is what 'total depravity' means—we are 'depraved' (not in the sense that we are debauched, but in the sense of the word's Latin root—all is somehow 'distorted') 'totally' (in everything).

So statesmen have to deal with self-centred men and women who are thus sinners; and what they have to provide is fundamentally security. This may surprise us. But the first priority of government is not so much love or justice, as 'some reasonable measure of security against murder, robbery, and starvation'.[19]

For that reason Temple was not so much interested in promises as in achievements. A system can promise a great deal, but if it cannot deliver the basic necessities of life it is useless. So he concluded: 'Its assertion of Original Sin should make the Church intensely realistic and conspicuously free from Utopianism.'[20]

It was for this reason that Temple never forgot the priority of evangelism and church growth: 'If we have to choose between making men Christian and making the social order more Christian, we must choose the former.'[21] But as we have seen, he obviously thought both were necessary.

9

Democracy and the Family

Christians in the United Kingdom have different views on what are economic and political priorities. However, most are united over the principle of democracy as it has evolved in our own constitution.

But is there anything essentially Christian about democracy, beyond promoting individual responsibility?

Democracy

As a matter of fact liberal democracy as we know it is a phenomenon that seems to have thrived on Christian soil. Some, however, argue that pluralism is essential for a democracy. It needs the combat of ideas and philosophies. It is held together, they say, not by a religious or ideological faith but by a practical faith. Some have called this a 'civic faith' or 'secular faith'. Jacques Maritain, a Roman Catholic political philosopher, in the post-war period expressed this point of view. He argued that 'men possessing quite different, even opposite metaphysical or religious outlooks' can meet together at a practical level, 'provided that they similarly revere, perhaps for quite diverse reasons, truth and intelligence, human dignity, freedom, brotherly love, and the absolute value of moral good'.[1]

But he must not be misunderstood. For Maritain was not wanting to cut the link between Christianity and democracy, for democracy itself, he believed, was 'a temporal manifestation of the inspiration of the gospel'. It was not that the Christian faith required you to be a democrat. But given Christianity, in time democracy was bound to arise.

The point he was making is this. Democracy is a solution to the problem of different views and conflicting values. In a democracy everybody has his say. A vote is taken. The matters are settled. But, Maritain would argue, if there is never a pluralism of different views and conflicting values, there is no need for discussion in the first place.

There is surely a certain truth in this. It is undoubtedly the case that the Parliamentary system in British history came about through conflicts of views and values. But while these were sometimes very strong, the disagreements, we can now see, were all under the 'sacred canopy' of the Christian world-view. The pluralism of views was a secondary or subordinate one; the disagreements, sometimes very strong, were within the 'civic faith' that the *Christian* faith nurtures.

But the doctrine of 'realism' and original sin does not allow us to be too hopeful that man, unaided by the grace of God, will always be good in these matters of 'truth and intelligence, human dignity, freedom, brotherly love, and the absolute value of moral good'. Since 1951, when Maritain wrote those words, the world has witnessed some awful atrocities—in Algeria, Nigeria, Vietnam, Cambodia, Uganda and many other places. Maritain's prized values have often been in conspicuously short supply.

As Maritain argues, a case can be made out, therefore, for democracy needing the seed bed of a Christian value system; given that value system, subordinate pluralisms give rise to democracy. But when that Christian value system is not being properly nurtured, there is no guarantee that liberal democracy can continue indefinitely. After all, it needs a great deal of commitment to function well. And it has yet to be proved that the civic faith can function well in a culture without the background of Christian faith.

Moral values and social functioning

But how democratic is Britain? Are the views and values of the people sufficiently expressed and heard in public? Does the overall ethos reflect majority wishes? Are those who communicate values representing national values or the values of the public at large?

As we have already said, we must not judge a society's ethos exclusively from the standpoint of individual beliefs. For the religious and moral-cultural system is embodied in institutions as well. We must be very careful, therefore, before we confine that system exclusively to what has been called 'the inner psyche or the privacy of conscience'. It is a fact that individuals, churches (congregations and denominations), universities, newspapers, publishers, television networks, political parties and the monarchy help to produce the overall ethos of our society.

We have argued that the constitution of the United Kingdom gives us, to a considerable degree, a Christian value system. But some of these other agencies clearly do not. But the democratic question is this: is the leadership in these institutions, and *especially in the media,* in touch with majority opinion on a number of the religious and moral-cultural issues? There is some evidence that it is not. If that is correct it is doubly necessary for the Christian voice to be heard again in these various public agencies or arenas.

This is not only in terms of justice, but in terms of the consequences of a further dilution of public ethics and values. For the question, as we have seen, is this: how long can our democracy and our economic order that goes with it (either democratic socialism or democratic capitalism) last when Christian values are no longer a vital force in the culture? And how long can these Christian values be maintained without the Christian faith being strong?

According to the Harris Poll in *The Spectator* (13th December 1986, p. 19), 'top people' in Britain appear to be more church-going than others. But as yet we have no definite figures relating to how far the views of those in institutional leadership and of influence in the media are representing those 'on the ground'. However, there are figures for the United States, and our experience is not totally divorced from theirs.

In 1981 Research and Forecasts of New York produced a *Report on American Values in the 80s.*[2] It had some important findings. Most significant were these: half of all Americans currently doubt that politics or economic policies alone can solve basic societal problems—crime, inflation and fundamental resource problems. It showed more than had been expected that people were turning to spiritual and religious commitments as the solution. It showed that religious values were number one on their order of priorities. 'Bewildered by the confusion of the present, large numbers of citizens now find solace in the firm conviction of their ancestors.'[3]

Interestingly, the report showed that these religious convictions have a direct bearing on economic values, especially work and the family. Here are some of the findings:

a) The 'most religious' Americans are more likely than the 'least religious' to feel a sense of dedication to their work (97% versus 66%);

b) The 'most religious' are more likely to find that their work contributes to society (91% versus 52%);

c) The 'most religious' are more likely to find their work interesting and rewarding (92% versus 68%);

d) The 'most religious' are more likely to believe financial security can be obtained by hard work (88% versus 70%);

e) The 'most religious' are much more likely to say they would reconcile marital problems at all costs rather than seek divorce (60% versus 33%).

Values in leadership

Now, of course, it might be argued that the 'most religious' belong to the elites that have the rewarding jobs in the first place and that these findings support the 'religion and the rise of capitalism' theory. But the findings suggested otherwise. Those holding stricter views were not found among the elites. This was certainly true of personal values. For the values associated with Christian personal ethics were not held so much by those in leadership positions and positions of public influence. Rather they were held more by the public at large. Here are the figures:

Leaders and the public at large on moral issues (in percentages):

Issues considered morally wrong	Public	Leaders	News media
Abortion	65	36	35
Homosexual practice	71	42	38
Lesbianism	70	42	37
Adultery	85	71	72
Premarital sex	40	31	20
Sex before 16	71	55	54
Cohabitation before marriage	47	32	24
Pornographic films	68	56	46
Hard drugs	84	73	66
Marijuana	57	33	22

But whatever people's beliefs may be in detail, the report made this clear: there is increasingly a public recognition that the spiritual and religious dimension to life is more basic to social and economic questions than the physical and political. The economist and newspaper columnist Warren Brookes commented that the report shows 'that spiritual values are fundamental to economic values; that goodness does have to do with the GNP'. But, he adds, 'Unfortunately, the study also found that on a whole range of specific moral issues, "American leaders are substantially out of tune with the public they are supposed to represent."'

The moral and ethical aspects of public life and culture in America, then, are being directed (particularly in the media) by leaders whose personal values do not necessarily reflect the moral currents of the public at large. The question we must ask is this—does this American experience mirror the experience of the United Kingdom? America can be a useful bell-wether for Europe and Great Britain.

The family

Moral and spiritual values are essential for the maintenance of an efficient social, economic and political order. But key among them are those that relate to the family and personal morality. The failure to focus on mediating structures in public life and society has meant that for a long time we have ignored the family. But commonsense makes it quite clear that a society is made up of much more than the individual on the one hand and the State on the other. But for a long time we have worked on the assumption that public policy can concern itself solely with individual protection and the maintenance of individual rights. We also assume that it is right for public policy to concern itself with the healthy functioning of the state and local government, and also with the economy. But we feel that family and sexual values are more private.

We must, of course, distinguish public policy from government interference. For example, it is perfectly possible for a society to say that adultery is wrong, without deciding then to stone the adulterer! A majority in a society may and probably should decide on legal tolerance for many matters of personal ethics with which it profoundly disagrees. But in the interests of the good of society, where it disagrees it should aim to make the reasons for its disagreements publicly known. It certainly should not be prevented from voicing its protests. Moral convictions publicly expressed are perfectly compatible with tolerance of alternative views.

No one can deny that the family and matters relating to sexual relationships have profound societal implications. 'Can business executives who routinely cheat on their spouses be expected not to cheat the consumer, the Government, or their competitors?' asks Warren Brookes.[4]

Even more serious are the consequences of illegitimate births. The Office of Population Censuses and Surveys revealed that illegitimate births in the United Kingdom increased from 55,000 in 1975 to 126,000 in 1985.[5] The Family Policies Studies Centre said in 1986 that more illegitimate children are born in the United Kingdom than in most of the rest of Europe. True, some of these are the result not just of 'accidents' but from couples living together. But even so those figures, along with the rising divorce rate, indicate the possibility of serious social problems. For can children born out of wedlock (and growing up in single-parent families) be expected to lead stable and productive lives when a large proportion of teenage crime may be traced to fatherless homes?[6]

It is the same with abortion. Can a society where one in five pregnancies end in abortion, and with that practice seeming to be more and more a routine form of birth control, be surprised when disregard for life results in various forms of violence?

No one can deny that family and sexual values and ethics are important. But they have been attacked in capitalist societies by those that have thought them of no public concern. They have also been attacked, even more strongly, by Marxists.

The family under attack

Marx, of course, never thought that the family was unimportant. In the Marxist tradition the family is to be ignored or opposed. 'The bourgeois clap trap about the family and education, about the hallowed relation of parent and child,' wrote Marx and Engels in *The Communist Manifesto*, 'becomes all the more disgusting, the more, by the action of Modern Industry, all family ties among the proletarians are torn asunder, and their children transformed into simple articles of commerce and instruments of labour.'[7] We can sympathize with this against the background of child labour that Shaftesbury succeeded in outlawing in the last century. But this view is still being repeated these days by modern day Marxists, even though children are now well protected by law. Here is a statement written in 1974 by R. D. Laing's associate, David Cooper:

> The bourgeois nuclear family (which in this context I shall henceforth refer to as 'the family') is the principal mediating device that the capitalist ruling class uses to condition the individual, through primary socialization, to fit into *some role complex* that suits the system.[8]

This argument may carry little conviction, but it is symptomatic of an onslaught on the family that has come from the left this century. The Russian dissident Igor Shafarevich, in his book *The Socialist Phenomenon*, explains that the Socialist project of homogenizing society demands that the family be vitiated or destroyed. This can be accomplished in good measure by profaning conjugal love and breaking monogamy's link between sex and loyalty. Hence, in their missionary phases Socialist movements often stress sexual 'liberation', and members of radical organizations may impose mandatory promiscuity within the group, everyone sharing a bed with each of the others, each equally related to each. It is the ultimate in leveling.[9]

Of course, as with much on the lunatic and enthusiastic fringes, the theory is unworkable. Society cannot function without a strong family and sexual ethic. So now in Moscow there has been an official line against the increase of prostitution in the city. In practice the family is discovered to be indispensable.

The Christian teaching on monogamous marriage is defined as a 'creation ordinance'. It has to do with man as such. It is not a 'perk' for believers, but it relates to how man is made, whether he recognizes it or not. The heterosexual ideal of one man and one woman for life can never be transcended. The models of homosexual relationships, one-parent families or serial marriage are wrong because they are not suited to human nature. They are to be opposed not because they are 'nasty' or 'naughty', but because they don't work. So Michael Novak, the Roman Catholic social scientist, writes:

Although there is much vocal contempt for the 'nostalgic family', few such critics seem really to propose that having one parent is superior to having two; that prodigal separation, divorce, and infidelity have only good effects; that coupling without marriage and marriage without children best serve the common good; or that the best of all societies would encourage an impermanent, childless, sexual free-for-all. The hostile critics of the family are shockingly vague about what they plan to put in its place, beyond 'liberation' and 'openness'.[10]

Family functions

From a social point of view the positive achievements of the family can be seen in three spheres—the economic, the political and the moral-cultural.

First, the economic achievements of the family can be illustrated by the experience of various ethnic groups. It has been argued that family strength is a factor in their relative economic performance. In the United Kingdom, for example, this may be seen in Indian communities that have tight family structures. This is one factor in their economic strength. In the United States 70% of all Jewish children between the ages of eighteen and twenty-two are in colleges or universities. Jews, of course, also have a very strong family system.

But even on a commonsense level the family is an economic asset. Members of the family help each other out with tasks and advice that would otherwise have to be paid for. Thus 'every single family network that becomes a centre of intelligent economic activity and a repository of hard-won economic habits is an immeasurable resource for the nation of which it is a part,' says Michael Novak.[11]

Furthermore, economic activity in many cases is stimulated by people working for their families. A sense of responsibility towards others in the family is probably more of a motivator for working and saving than working and saving for one's self. But most important of all, the family creates a sense of economic balance. 'If the family is a form of socialism which corrects the exaggerated individualism of capitalist economists, it is also a form of liberty which corrects the exaggerated collectivism of statists,' says Novak.[12]

Secondly, there are the political achievements of the family. These are less obvious. But a case can be made out for saying that strong families are essential for democratic self-government. 'It is in the family that the habits of mind and will indispensable to the conception and practice of self-government are best taught—only there can be taught. If individuals have no space protecting them from the state, they have no "self" for self-government.'[13]

Thirdly, there is the moral-cultural dimension. In this we may put the achievements of the family during the 'nurture' period. This is a period of anything up to twenty years. During that time many of the fruits of the inherited culture have to be transmitted to the next generation. It is also during this period in families that religious belief is taught and fostered.

There is also the provision of security during this nurture period. But this is what is at risk with the rise in illegitimate births, even though half of them are to parents living together at the time. This in itself indicates a serious problem. As Professor Whitfield says, 'There appears to be reticence or a fear of commitment between these partners which, at the very least, does not promote the security and identity, legal and otherwise, which is generally helpful for all parents and children.'[14]

He also makes the point that 'the overall costs to the public purse, and to industry, of the consequences of household turmoil and insecurity, however caused, are vast.' And this may be unacceptable at some point, he argues, to the main political parties. But this failure to make and sustain 'long-term promises to our mates' is in danger of becoming 'fashionable'. And he continues:

A key to healthy development throughout the life cycle is to know that we are individually significant, that we are intrinsically valuable to at least a few others whose sustained love and acceptance we experience. The foundations of such conviction, of a secure identity and the related capacity to share in love and commitment, are laid down in childhood; they are often intergenerationally transmitted, which bequeathes no small challenge for teaching.

And so the conclusion is that 'family formation and maintenance lie at the heart of creating viable societies'. Consequently these issues should immediately 'be far more central in the nation's business'.

Discipline and guidance

Related to this as far as the moral-cultural order is concerned, are discipline and guidance. These are among the most important achievements of the family. In strong families children learn the value of discipline and self-discipline. For families can only function when there is a measure of order. Thus the breakdown of discipline and the breakdown of the family in Western society are two sides of the same coin. The trouble lies to some extent with the generation of parents born between the wars. They were influenced by various theories that linked discipline to repression, and so fell over backwards not to be authoritarian and judgemental. The result is now moral paralysis and confusion.

A rather sad article appeared in *The Times* written by a mother who found her son regularly bringing his girlfriend home and sleeping with her:

> I have not said anything, nor has my husband. Indeed, what could we possibly say? . . . Looking back, I believe that my son would have been genuinely surprised and taken aback if I had raised an objection about his girlfriend staying the night. But I simply wouldn't have known what opinions or sanctions I could have offered.[15]

There can be no doubt that weak families offering little in the way of guidelines or discipline are damaging to individuals and the state.

According to the President of the National Association of Head Teachers some children can hardly speak when they start school simply because their parents do not talk to them at home. Mrs Jeanne Leake told delegates at the Association's conference in May 1986 that there were now children in infant classes with a total lack of experience needed for language development. They had no stories, no nursery rhymes, no physical contact with adults, and no cultural background. 'Children are aggressive because they have been isolated and had no social training.' Parental responsibility for their own children must be top priority, she added. 'Far too often children are left abandoned to their own devices in homes both affluent and poor. But long-term unemployment had led to the break-up of marriages,' she said. 'The ease of obtaining divorces and re-marriages contributes to children being at risk.' Good family relationships were essential to the well-being of children, she concluded, and the failure of adults to establish relationships must have a backlash.[16]

10

A Tale of Two Men

The Head of Religious Broadcasting at the BBC, Colin Morris, has talked about 'a revolutionary take-over of society accomplished without a shot being fired'. And the local agent of the revolution, he says, 'sits demurely in your sitting-room, staring at you glassy-eyed—your television set'.[1] No understanding of society in Britain would be complete without reference to broadcasting; and there is no way we can talk about moral-cultural values and the place of Christianity in the Public Square without talking about how the church should relate to the electronic media.

The revolution

The revolution has undoubtedly been subtle. For it is not always the outrageous, the blasphemous or the overtly biased Radio and TV programmes that bring about cultural change and dislodge tried and tested values. But as David Winter, the Head of Religious Programmes BBC Radio, says: 'The main impact of television is not through single programmes, however controversial or newsworthy, but through the steady trickle of attitudes, views and opinions.'[2] It is undoubtedly the case that programmes like *Woman's Hour* or *The World at One* or any of the other 'safe' magazine programmes have enormous influence in legitimizing attitudes and views and thus effecting cultural change. So the electronic media have become a basic constituent in the formation of a public consciousness. Radio and TV have extended the frontiers of the Public Square or Public Forum. Currently, in the United Kingdom, however, the Christian community experiences a certain exclusion, if not opposition, from the existing broadcasting establishments. But how on earth has that happened? In part it is 'the tale of two men'—John Reith and Hugh Greene.

It is now readily admitted that humanism is the creed of many in broadcasting while Christianity is *passé*. One senior BBC drama producer said rather cynically that in broadcasting today you can be committed to anything except Christianity. Colin Morris seems to agree with the proposition that 'humanism in one form or another is probably the unacknowledged faith of the vast majority of broadcasters'.[3] David Winter says, 'Secular humanists virtually ran TV drama in the sixties and early seventies.'[4] And add to that the fact that some with enormous programme or editorial control in *religious* programming need have little or no Christian allegiance.

Yet when some of these same people (with views other than Christian) visit or work in Broadcasting House in London, as they walk in they see the dedicatory inscription (in Latin). When it is translated it is found to be full of biblical and Christian allusions:

> This temple of the arts and muses is dedicated to Almighty God by the first Governors of Broadcasting in the year 1931, Sir John Reith being Director General. It is their prayer that good seed sown may bring forth a good harvest; that all things hostile to peace and purity may be banished from this house and that the

people inclining their ear to whatsoever things are beautiful and honest and of good report may tread the path of wisdom and uprightness.

Here were obviously Christian ideals. But at a certain point in time the values at the BBC changed.

John Reith

The founding father of British broadcasting was John Reith. An engineer and brought up in a Scottish manse, he believed in God and he believed in guidance. In October 1922 he heard a sermon at Regent Square Church on the text in Ezekiel, 'Thus saith the Lord, "I sought a man to stand in the gap . . ."' That night he wrote in his diary, 'I still believe there is some great work for me to do in the world.' He then saw in the papers an advertisement for the job of 'general manager' for a company involved in what was called 'broadcasting'. He applied, realized the significance of the task, was offered the job, and again wrote in his diary, 'I had kept my faith alive: night and morning had comforted and encouraged myself with the words, "Commit thy way unto the Lord, trust also in Him and He shall bring it to pass".'[5] Here was a man who believed he had a divine destiny.

Morris summarizes the avowed aim of the British Broadcasting Company under Reith as 'the attempt to bring the best of everything into the greatest possible number of homes'.[6] Unashamedly he gave the Christian religion prominence. 'Christianity,' Reith said, 'happens to be the stated and official religion of the country; it is recognized by the Crown. This is a fact which those who have criticized our right to broadcast the Christian religion would do well to bear in mind . . .'[7]

But it was not only Reith who saw that the values of the BBC were to be Christian values. Twenty-five years later in 1948 the then Director-General, Sir William Haley, could still say this to the British Council of Churches:

> There are many demands of impartiality laid on the Corporation, but this [about Christian values] is not one of them. We are citizens of a Christian country and the BBC—an institution set up by the State—bases its policy upon a positive attitude towards the Christian values. It seeks to safeguard those values and to foster acceptance of them. The whole preponderant weight of its programmes is directed towards this end.[8]

But by 1965 'humanism' had taken over! The Director-General of the day, Sir Hugh Greene, also knew there could be no neutrality in broadcasting. But he seemed to be saying (subtly) the values were only going to be those of liberal humanism. He would not be impartial where 'there are clashes for and against the basic moral values, truthfulness, justice, freedom, compassion, tolerance. Nor do I believe we should be impartial about certain things like racialism or extreme forms of political belief.'[9]

And the freedom (subtly) became 'freedom from positive Christian values'. But as we have seen, a freedom *from* positive Christian values may look like benign tolerance; but it is not neutral. It can be the suppression of these religious values and the denial of their clear statement; often it is the positive assertion of the religion of humanism. Of course, in themselves all these humanistic values are excellent and necessary. So is oxygen. But when you are dying of thirst it has got to be combined with hydrogen. The point is this: values do not work like 'half a loaf'. They are more like a chemical compound. Certain combinations are necessary for them to be viable in society.

But who decided that a positive attitude towards full Christian values should be replaced by a reductionist form of basic moral values? Who said that a majority in the country did not still think that Christian values were essential for maintaining moral values? Hugh Greene himself, it seems. But, if so and to be fair, this was in exactly the same way that

Reith unilaterally decided he would maintain a Christian position.

Something is surely wrong with a monopoly (or duopoly of the BBC and IBA) that gives such power for reinforcing or restructuring the moral-cultural order to single individuals or to groups of individuals.

TeleVision North

However, the rights and wrongs of the matter are secondary at present (although Reith could argue he was doing nothing other than was appropriate for a state institution, given our national constitution). The serious consequence *now* for the nation is this. The 'concordat' in British broadcasting with the Christian community was established under Lord Reith's reign, not Hugh Greene's. And the churches were generally happy with that arrangement. It is now, however, quite another matter under a predominantly humanist broadcasting establishment.

Indeed, it is intolerable that the Christian community finds itself gagged. For it represents (constitutionally) the values of the nation and also represents what appears to be the preference of a majority. But it is not able to enjoy freely the responsible expression of views and values via the electronic media. Such limited expression as it is permitted is courtesy of an overall humanistic editorial and programming policy. Furthermore, 'religious' broadcasters in the establishment, good and Christian as they may be, have no responsibility to the Christian community itself, only to what seems to have become a humanistic broadcasting hierarchy, with all the pressures that can bring.

Given the history of the recent past it will be argued that the clock cannot be put back. The conventional argument is, therefore, that Christians should now 'get involved'. But involved in what? It is necessary, but not sufficient, to tell

Christians of ability to become researchers, producers and broadcasters. First, that is because there are not always openings. Secondly, creative skills are of little avail if the policy decisions higher up are often frustrating.

Nor is it sufficient, although necessary, to tell Christians with political skills to be involved in applying for franchises for the regions of independent television and radio to help change these policy decisions. They can be, they are and, at the level of social responsibility, they should be. But this does not give much of a Christian voice in the public forum that radio and television have created.

At the last redistribution of franchises I myself convened a consortium to bid for the north-east television region, Tele-Vision North (TVN); we were partially successful in that along with the other two applicants, Tyne Tees and Norse-man, we all were offered a third stake in a new contracting company. TVN refused, as we wanted all or nothing.

But this was not a company to promote Christian views. It was a modest attempt by those of us who were Christian at social responsibility. It was a piece of social leavening, not Christian witness. But the present system manages not only to frustrate the latter (Christian witness) but even the former (Christian social responsibility).

The goal of this application company was twofold: one, simply to provide better television for the north-east (that does not mean elitist television) and, two, to take financial control out of the hands of Trident Television. As the company controlling Yorkshire Television, they had bought-up Tyne Tees in the mid-seventies; and such profits as could be ploughed back into north-east television seemed to be going out of the region into ventures like Windsor Safari Park. Some of us wanted more money put back locally.

The company (TVN) would have involved very distinguished people on the board and some prestigious programme makers on the books. With a turnover of £20 million it would have made a significant contribution to the northeast and the network.

But such is the moral-cultural climate in broadcasting today that you have to apologize for being a Christian! It seemed there was prejudice in certain quarters because some of us were associated with the church. I myself was a clergyman; the prospective programme controller, formerly in the BBC Schools' Television department, a director of *Panorama,* acting editor of *The Money Programme,* executive producer of *Visnews* and so on, was a committed Christian. It didn't matter that the chairman, Sir Monty Finniston, was a Jew, one of the team of new programme makers was a Buddhist, and financial control was under the eye of a worldly-wise former member of the IBA itself!

The fact that two of the putative board members were known to be committedly Christian seemed to be a hindrance. If I had destroyed another man's family life by seducing and running off with his wife, if as a chairman of a big business I had ruthlessly destroyed some small business, causing suffering, hardship and unemployment, if I had advocated homosexual practice, abortion on demand, and general sexual licence, I probably would have been less handicapped than having to say I was Vicar of Jesmond! Something is radically wrong, sick and in need of change as far as the broadcasting establishment and its connections is concerned.

Cable

So there clearly has to be change. And the Peacock Report of July 1986 suggests the way forward: deregulation, but with subsidized Public Service Broadcasting still to provide services that otherwise would be edged out by market forces. But with such deregulation it is imperative that Christian groups have at last full access to television channels and radio broadcasting frequencies—of course, properly limited by the laws of the land and the constraints of the market place. Already this is what the Government has come to see is right, as has the church.

On February 10th, 1983, the General Synod of the Church of England discussed the proposals for the development of Cable systems and services, on the basis of the Hunt Report and a Government White Paper. The Hunt Report and the White Paper (drawn up in the light of the report) wanted to exclude the church from this new technology!

The Synod, however, said 'No' for the church thought it right and just to have *direct* access to any new systems. It voted, in fact, for the 'participation of churches and other religious bodies in the ownership of cable operating companies and the opportunity for such religious bodies to own or lease individual channels'. This resolution was forwarded to the Government.

The House of Commons then debated the White Paper. In the debate the Labour MP, Donald Anderson, made the following important point: 'Just as in the past it would have been intolerable if churches had been excluded from the printing press, so it would be intolerable now if churches were excluded from such future television developments.' Mr Anderson said that the argument that extremist sects like the Moonies might take over channels was overstated. They had not done so in the United States. Such sects need to develop 'dependency' situations. These he believed could not be achieved by television.[10]

The result of these and other arguments was that when the new Cable Bill appeared it was drafted so as to allow Christian groups to be able to participate in the ownership of operating companies (although not have a controlling share) and such bodies can own or lease individual channels. The Cable Authority is simply there to ensure 'that *undue* prominence is not given in the programmes to the views and opinions of particular persons or bodies on religious matters (or matters of political or industrial controversy or relating to current public policy)'.

This is a significant development. It has been unheralded as cable is hardly viable or profitable as yet. But it is obviously the beginning of a new move. An important principle has been established, although there is a long way to go.

The sixties

Deregulation is the price that now has to be paid after the Reithian 'Christian consensus' was abandoned in favour of an aggressive and exclusivist humanism. But how did that radical change in broadcasting values come about?

It happened during the sixties. It is difficult to prove whether this change reflected certain trends outside the broadcasting establishment or was the cause of these trends. A good case can be made out for saying that the broadcasters were the prime movers. If so the three culprits were the financial success of the new Independent TV companies; the advent of BBC2 in 1964 and the policies of Hugh Greene, appointed Director-General in 1959.

It was soon discovered that commercial companies were 'a licence to print money'. After that night on September 22nd, 1955, when Sir John Barbirolli and the prestigious Hallé Orchestra played at the opening of the first Independent Television channel, the companies never really looked back. There have been nervous moments since and some disasters, but all in all it has been commercially comfortable.

But the success of ITV meant that the BBC had to do something different to regain audiences. So they tried 'social realism', which meant an absence of social graces and a surfeit of bad language. It also involved a piece of what looked like sheer 'Southern' arrogance. The assumption seemed to be that if you lived in the North of England your interests did not lie further than beer, bingo and betting shops. And *Z Cars* replaced *Dixon of Dock Green* (your friendly local 'bobby'); the Police were now identified as tough, rough and cynical. But social realism paid off in terms of audience ratings. The price, however, some said, was not worth it; for the mores of the BBC *did* affect society.

The second important factor in the sixties was the opening of a second BBC channel. The Pilkington Committee's Report in 1962 came down on the side of the BBC and against the ITV companies. This was important, for what was at stake was the granting of another channel. Who was to have a second string to their bow? The BBC or ITV? In the end the BBC were awarded it and 1964 saw the advent of BBC 2.

The significance of BBC 2 was more in terms of the management problem it caused. For all of a sudden you had to increase the pool of broadcasters by (potentially) 50%. At times like the inauguration of a new channel or a redistribution of the franchises there is a certain amount of 'musical chairs' in terms of filling jobs and posts. But it is obvious that a new channel actually needs more people. And the advent of BBC 2 meant that many young people, often from Oxford and Cambridge, had to be taken on board in disproportionate numbers. Also, promotion came earlier and younger to some others already in the BBC. The net result was a great influx or promotion of creative people who had not learned the Reith ways. Add to that the fact that outside—in the moral-cultural sphere—it was a 'low' in the church's life. This was before the new evangelicalism had really taken effect. It was the hey-day of the 'new theology' of *Honest to God* by Bishop John Robinson and *The Death of God* theologians. All was ripe for an explosion. The match that lit the touch paper was Hugh Greene.

Hugh Greene

So the third factor that lead to the change of values in the sixties was undoubtedly the very able, very shrewd, but somewhat biased Hugh Charlton Greene. He was an expert in the psychological manipulation of the media. He had masterminded the BBC's broadcasts to Nazi Germany during the war and headed up the Psychological Warfare Department in Malaya during the emergency. He was a professional. Whether you want men like this at a time when 'winning back the viewers' is a priority is questionable. Not every method is legitimate.

But Greene understood what makes people tick. The *Wednesday Plays, Steptoe and Son* and *Till Death us do Part* were all creations of the Greene era and were huge successes. They gave huge offence, too. The problem was that in the sixties there was a great amount of remarkable, inventive and creative talent among broadcasters. But it lacked the constraints of an agreed value system. Much expressed itself in the form of criticism of the existing social order. It was probably not Marxist, though some said it was. Rather it was a statement that society was sick. It was. Indeed, we were witnessing the frenzied last rites of an era that was coming to an end—an era of 'Enlightenment' that went back two centuries. Maybe the sixties had to happen. Maybe it was cathartic. But if so, we now need to look ahead towards reconstruction.

So Greene was the very opposite of Reith. Reith himself said so (in his diary): 'Hugh and I were fundamentally in complete opposition of outlook and attitude. I lead; he follows the crowd in all the disgusting manifestations of the age . . . Without any reservation he gives the public what it wants; I would not, did not and said I wouldn't.'[11]

But Reith had misjudged Greene. For Greene *was* trying to be ahead of public opinion. He generated permissiveness.

He was a leader in the new ways. In Rome in 1965 he said this:

> In its search for truth, indeed in whatever it undertakes, a broadcasting organization must recognize an obligation towards tolerance and towards the maximum liberty of expression . . . I believe that broadcasters have a duty not to be diverted by arguments in favour of what is, in fact, disguised censorship. I believe we have a duty to take account of the changes in society, *to be ahead of public opinion rather than always to wait upon it* . . . relevance is the key—relevance to the audience and to the tide of opinion in society. Outrage is impermissible. Shock is not always so. Provocation may be healthy and indeed socially imperative [italics mine—author].[12]

In fact Greene had taken a completely cavalier approach. He told a meeting on November 13th, 1963, that even if the Government had viewed his appointment 'with the utmost distaste, there was nothing they could do about it'. On another occasion in Middlesbrough, he boasted to his audience that 'we have never taken into account any notice of minority groups and the Governors are beginning to ignore them as well'.[13]

It is not therefore surprising that in time he worried Mrs Mary Whitehouse because of allowing too much sex and violence on television. He worried his successor as Director-General (at that time Secretary to the BBC), Charles Curran. Curran later described what he termed Hugh Greene's 'freewheeling and not particularly caring' attitude towards his job. And he worried his Chairman, Lord Normanbrook, who thought that Greene had 'an excessive attachment to libertarianism'. So by 1966 it was decided by Normanbrook that Greene should go, but Normanbrook died before he could get rid of Greene. However, Greene wrote to the woman who was to become his third wife that he 'was very fond of [Normanbrook]'. He certainly did not say that of Normanbrook's successor, Lord Hill. Hill had moved over from the ITA (now IBA) to the BBC with the job of 'sorting things out'. And that meant Greene obviously had to go. So he went.

Greene was either someone who brought the BBC out into the open air of the sixties; or he was someone who actually began to destroy Public Service Broadcasting as a national monopoly or duopoly. He probably did both. For with Christian consensus broadcasting brilliantly demolished by Greene, there was now an inevitable consequence. However reluctantly, influential sections of the Christian community would be demanding a new and independent deal.

II

Hidden Censors

It was William Temple who said that 'the intolerance of rationalists is quite as deep as that of traditionalists, and if its weapon is contempt rather than persecution, that is at once more irritating to the victim and far more spiritually corrupting to him who indulges in it'.[1] And that is still true today where there is a rationalist or humanist ethos; and such an ethos you have in broadcasting. There this intolerance leads to a subtle form of censorship. We have solved the problem of censorship with regard to the printing press. We now have to solve it with regard to Radio and TV.

The invention of printing was immediately used by the church to publish Bibles. But by the time of the Reformation the Roman Catholic Church was exercising a tight censorship over printing to control the spread of Protestant ideas. The Church of England also exercised censorship during the Elizabethan period. Material had to be vetted before it was published. But it was Milton in the *Areopagitica* who argued for a free press. In 1694, when Parliament refused to renew the Licensing Act, prepublication censorship came to an end. Macaulay described this as a greater contribution to liberty and civilization than either the Magna Carta or the Bill of Rights.[2] Of course, publications were subject to the laws of the land regarding sedition, blasphemy, obscenity and libel. But ideas were free.

Now in the electronic age we have a new censorship over broadcasting. But unlike the earlier censorship that was exercised by the church, this can go unnoticed. But it is nonetheless real. For whether we like it or not, the broadcasting establishment sometimes acts like a censor. It functions in a different way to earlier censors, but the end result is the same: it is the limitation of values that do not fit in with the censor's own values. And these, as we have seen, are too often of a secular humanist nature. The Government of Mrs Thatcher says they are also left wing.

Inherent problems

But we must be fair. Gone are the days of Hugh Greene. There is a new 'religious' mood in the country. More people now want to listen to the Sunday Morning Service on BBC Radio 4 than programmes like *The World this Weekend* and *Pick Of the Week*. BBC Religious Radio is doing better under David Winter. He writes:

> We're constantly told that this is a post-Christian, secular age, so why are so many more people busily listening to programmes about religion, which is supposedly redundant? My guess is that these statistics back up the impression created by correspondence, telephone calls and week by week contact with listeners —that the tide of interest in religious belief and experience is *rising,* not falling.[3]

So shouldn't we expect this to be reflected in the philosophy of our broadcasting? Is it quite so humanist today? Is it left wing? Probably things are changing, but we have a long way to go.

For we have to realize that it is perfectly possible for

people to be promoting humanistic (or disproportionately left-wing) views without there being any conspiracy to do so. This is something both the churches and the politicians must realize.

On the religious side, the broadcasters' desire for 'balance' may be one of the factors that unconsciously produces an unrepresentative pluralism. This in turn reinforces a basic humanist philosophy. And the total message that is then heard from the studio as far as religious values are concerned is: one, that there is a premium on religious 'tentativeness'; two, that conviction is discounted; and, three, that 'faith' is a matter of shopping between competing ideologies. Now, that may be acceptable for a religion such as Hinduism, but not for Christianity.

On the political side, it may be inevitable that broadcasting seems left-wing to a right-wing Government and vice-versa. Because of the nature of news gathering the incumbent party will always be subject to investigation in a way that opposition parties are not. Even the best of Governments are still imperfect; so there will always be some failures to report. Sadly such is the nature of life in the West that good news is 'no news' while bad news is definitely 'news'. Thus there is a tendency for the news simply to be criticism of the Government. The opposition parties, being more out of the news, have an easier ride.

But there is another factor that leads the media to appear to be biased against open and free societies, and thus politically on the left; yet this is not necessarily the case and it is a misleading impression. Sir Robin Day drew attention to this when he said, 'One of T.V.'s *inherent* limitations is that its coverage contains a built-in bias against free and open societies. T.V. is far more able to give a critical and unflattering picture of a free society than of any totalitarian one.' This, he explained, was simply because you are not allowed to make films in totalitarian states. So he concluded:

This cannot fail to have a profound effect on public opinion in free countries where T.V. is *the* mass medium of news and information. The public is constantly reminded in the most vivid way of the evils in its own society and in those other countries where T.V. is free to prowl. But the evils of life in closed totalitarian countries cannot be given anything like the same emphasis. All of which tends to lead to a grossly distorted view of the world.[4]

It therefore appears as if the media is biased against Western capitalism and is in favour of collectivist Marxism!

Commercialism

But whatever the truth about intentions, all this adds up to a strong case for not letting a privileged elite be the arbiters as to what information is to be selected for communication through the electronic media. Nor, as we have said, does this imply any conspiracy theory. Broadcasters can simply be *unconscious* of the way their message is received by the general public. Various factors may distort the 'signals'.

In Britain we are now at the point where there has to be 'consumer sovereignty'. As Tony Benn has well said, 'Broadcasting is too important to leave to the broadcasters.' But there are a number of other problems and distortions that have to be faced from the churches' side. There is, of course, the naked materialism that television especially represents. Malcolm Muggeridge tells of how he once took Mother Teresa to a New York television studio for a breakfast show. It was the first time she had been to an American television studio, and so, said Muggeridge,

> she was quite unprepared for the constant interruptions for commercials. As it happened, surely as a result of divine intervention, all the commercials that particular morning were to do with different varieties of packaged food, recommended as being non-fattening and non-nourishing. Mother Teresa looked

at them with a kind of wonder, her own constant preoccupation being, of course, to find the where-with-all to nourish the starving and put some flesh on human skeletons. It took some little time for the irony of the situation to strike her. When it did, she remarked, in a perfectly audible voice: 'I see that Christ is needed in television studios.' A total silence descended on all present.[5]

There is a serious problem for communication now that television is a main medium. And that, very simply, is this: television is conditioned by money. And money is only forthcoming if people watch programmes. The temptation, therefore, to cut moral corners in the interests of ratings is enormous. Nor is it any good saying that we want to be above money. Television is a very expensive exercise. Money has to be generated. To put Mother Teresa on the air costs money. But as with paying tribute to Caesar, it seems to be compromising, paying for her with enticements to breakfast cereals that nobody wants. But maybe this is part of the fallenness of the world; until there is a total spiritual renewal Caesar will still continue to behave in a certain way and have the equivalent of engraven coins! But if so, the Christian community has to be on its guard.

Fantasy and reality

Muggeridge, however, seems to believe we need a stronger reaction. He seems to think that television broadcasting is almost irredeemable as a means of communication. There are at least three reasons.

First 'the medium is the message'—the medium defines the message and it is seductive. It presents fantasy, not reality. Muggeridge gives us a powerful parable in his book, *Christ and the Media*. It is the fourth temptation. Jesus, having successfully countered Satan three times in the wilderness, is now offered a contract from Lucifer Inc. to go to

Rome and anchor a chat show. 'For the set they'd have fountains playing, a lush atmosphere, with organ music, a good chorus-line, if possible from Delphi, and some big names from the games.'

But Jesus is 'concerned with truth and reality' rather than 'fantasy and images' and so refuses. He was concerned with an altogether more significant 'scenario . . . the great drama of the Incarnation, the Passion and the Resurrection'. The message of that was carried 'without benefit of media, first from Judea to Asia Minor, and thence to Europe to spread through the whole Roman Empire'. As a direct result, across the centuries the greatest artists, architects, poets, musicians and mystics have 'dedicated their genius to celebrating it'. That, says Muggeridge, is communication.[6]

Secondly, there is a fear that television can create social realities. And it clearly does. Many demonstrations are arranged for the sake of exposure on television. Jerry Rubin, speaking from personal experience in numerous demonstrations has admitted that 'on the television screen news is not so much reported as created'.[7]

Thirdly, television's power can be degrading and dehumanizing. Muggeridge cites 'a horrifying example' from the Biafran War in Nigeria. An execution was to take place. Just as the command to fire was about to be given a cameraman cried 'Cut!'—his battery had gone dead and needed replacing. The execution waited until the battery was fitted. The cameraman shouted, 'Action!'; then shots were fired and the prisoner fell down dead, 'his death duly recorded, to be shown in millions of sitting rooms throughout the so-called civilized world'.[8]

Muggeridge's warnings should be heeded, even though he may sometimes exaggerate. John Stott was chairing the London Lectures in Contemporary Christianity at which Muggeridge expressed all these ideas. In his chairman's speech he likened Malcolm Muggeridge to a prophet and thanked God for him but went on, 'Sometimes prophets exaggerate.' He mentioned Elijah, who thought he alone was left alive, when there were 7,000 others!

Nevertheless the distortion, manipulation, and insensitivity that is associated with TV is another reason why we must call a halt to the control of this very dangerous medium by what seems an unrepresentative, privileged elite.

Distortions

But there are two other factors that mean that the present system of control (or censorship) by the broadcasting establishments must be checked.

First, and perhaps the most serious of all, is a factor that is unique to television. David Winter sums it up like this:

> When you read a report in a newspaper, or hear it on the radio, you know that what you are hearing is *another person's* view of an event or situation. Consequently you treat it as what it is—a second-hand experience of the event.
>
> But television gives me the illusion of actually being there. I am at the picket line. I watch the police struggling with Orange marchers. I am not aware of any intermediary: seeing is believing.[9]

But, of course, unknown to us, we are seeing the event in a selected and edited fashion. David Winter says that the trouble is that in the credits we don't have included such lines as:

> Researcher: Jill Nobbs (neo-Trot) . . . Producer: John Carbon (one time NF Organizer) . . . Reporter: Julia Nowall (president of Troops Out Balham branch).

'Yet,' he says, 'without that kind of knowledge, one is taking an awful lot on trust.'

Secondly, there is the fact that many of the best documentaries or social comment programmes are 'crusading'—

like the classic and brilliant *Cathy Come Home* of the Greene era. And so they should be. But is it not very dangerous in a democracy to allow a small, unelected, privileged group to decide exclusively what crusades to wage on behalf of society?

And broadcasters and producers of documentaries can come to a situation with their minds made up. Martin Carr, a veteran producer of documentaries on all three main American networks, said as much in 1978. He confessed that the producer's first step was to 'arrive at a point of view'. Balance had to be maintained but maintained carefully; otherwise you upset the 'emotional impact' of the programme. He explained how you might first interview someone as an opponent to your position. But if his personality would charm the viewers, you have to go for someone else who would alienate. Referring to a specific programme, Carr reports, 'One could only feel a particular way at the end of the film . . . the way I felt about it!'[10]

Related to this is what has been called 'the Pinsky Principle', after an American journalist, Walter Pinsky. He described his approach in the *Columbia Journalism Review* in 1976: 'If my research and journalistic instincts tell me one thing, my political instincts another . . . I won't fudge it, I won't bend it, but I won't write it.'[11]

Now, these problems affect all television programmes of a report, analysis or documentary nature. But they do not only affect *non*-religious programmes. For different values or theologies affect also religious broadcasting.

Here is a description of 'a sample Sunday's broadcasting'. It was from the period of Yorkshire Television's *Stars on Sunday,* which was described as 'the depths of vulgarity' and 'showbiz religion'. Its message was simple:

> It is the reverse of guilt by association. If God is good enough for Gracie Fields, he's good enough for you. These pious thespians serve up a brand of religion which can be guaranteed not

to spill over into social action. They are doing very nicely, thank you, out of our present society, so why would they want to rock the boat? They are shining examples of the truth that it is possible to have Jesus and two Rolls-Royces.

The other lot show a majestic, almost suicidal disdain for ratings. They run something called BBC Religious Television—80 minutes of blank screen punctuated by bursts of intellectual snobbery (who will forget that magic night they discussed Icelandic creation myths?) and bathetic nostalgia, viz. *Songs of Praise*.[12]

That acerbic (but uncomfortably near-the-bone) description of religious television came, in 1972, from Colin Morris, minister of Wesley's Chapel, City Road in London. Six years later he was himself appointed Head of Religious Broadcasting at the BBC. Eight years on *Songs of Praise* was still with us!

Religious broadcasting

It was the Archbishop of Canterbury, Randall Davidson, who first called together church leaders at the House of Lords to form a Sunday Committee. It later became known as the Central Religious Advisory Committee (CRAC) to discuss broadcasting affairs. John Reith had been able to persuade the Archbishop of the importance of Radio for the church.

Under Reith's guidance a substantial amount of programming developed. But a lot has happened since those days. The current guidelines for religious broadcasting are those laid down by CRAC in 1977:

1. To seek to reflect the worship, thought and action of the principal religious traditions represented in Britain, recognizing that these traditions are mainly though not exclusively Christian;
2. To seek to present to viewers and listeners those beliefs,

ideas, issues and experiences in the contemporary world which are evidently related to a religious interpretation or dimension of life;

3. To seek also to meet the religious interests, concerns and needs of those on the fringe of, or outside, the organized life of the Churches.

Some may not be surprised at Colin Morris's description of the BBC's Religious Television. But whether this 'brief' is a cause or a consequence, the reality is that religious television (if not BBC religious radio) seems to cut little ice. This is partly because it is too 'laid back'. Yet this comes from the pressure of the broadcasting services, being under a duopoly and so requiring 'balance'. So an easy way out for the broadcasters is not to have anything that needs balancing in the first place!

And that is the reason why there *must* be a multiplication of outlets and why Christians *must* determine their own programming without editorial censorship. The public can then choose what *it* wants. If it wants a clear expression or insight into positive Christianity, it can then get it. But if it wants establishment religious programming, it should still be able to get that from Public Service Broadcasting (according to Peacock).

The church owes it to the nation and to itself to preach the gospel of God via the electronic media. That is not naive partisanship. Lord Ramsey, the former Archbishop of Canterbury, had a much tighter view of religious television than the CRAC definition of 1977. He once told Kenneth Harris that religious television should help the committed Christian to 'an intelligent and thoughtful commitment instead of an unintelligent one, a commitment that has more thought of obligation to all those outside'.

Indeed, it is hard to see, unless there is a strong level of commitment, how you can have a programme that can sustain any interest. Whatever reservations some may have about the Americans and what has been called The Electronic Church, some of the material from the other side of the Atlantic is undeniably good television; and it is compulsive viewing. Nor is that because of any mesmeric effects, but because these American communicators believe what they are preaching and they are preaching to convert. Who is going to watch a programme where the programme stance is, 'I don't know if this is true and I'm not bothered whether you think it is true or not; that is not my brief. All I am to do is to reflect, present and meet religious interests'?

Exclusion

On so many counts something must be done. The writing was on the wall in 1983. The IBA, for example, in that year ignored CRAC's advice about programme scheduling. Until 1976 the BBC and ITV were bound by the convention that they would compete 'back to back' with religious programmes during the closed period of 6.15 pm and 7.25 pm on Sundays. The BBC, with the agreement of CRAC, broke the convention by transferring its religious comment programme to late evening. This concession was probably unwise on CRAC's part. In time the independent companies would want to follow suit. For the BBC seemed to be scheduling hard against the ITV's remaining religious programme to catch viewers. The BBC thus downgraded its own religious output and then forced its competitors to downgrade theirs.

The details needn't concern us. The issue proved what many had been saying for years—that CRAC was impotent, money determined everything and religious values could be censored out at the whim of a programme controller. As the head of Religious Programmes at Television South wrote in a letter to *The Times* (responding to a leading article):

Of course, the issue now goes far beyond this particular problem and you rightly call for urgent attention to it by both IBA and

BBC Governors. But it is for the churches, too, to make an urgent and severe reappraisal of their relationship with the two authorities. For too long they have accepted client status as the unspoken price of their protected position: but it is to them in the end that producers and Governors alike look to insist that this simply is not good enough.[13]

But nothing has been done. So, by 1986, for example, on a July Sunday all you had on the BBC was Colin Morris introducing forty-five minutes of *Sunday Worship* in the morning and in the evening thirty-five minutes of Cliff Michelmore in *Home on Sunday* talking to a Cornish poet. On ITV there was an hour of *Morning Worship* and thirty-five minutes at the time of the evening religious slot of Harry Secombe in *Highway,* according to the *TV Times* 'performing a song and dance routine with Billy Dainty in the first of five sentimental journeys to meet old friends and present a selection of viewers' past favourites'. And that was all—no late evening or early afternoon material as there was supposed to be; but in the north-east on Tyne Tees we had five minutes in the early morning of primary school children singing *Keyman* and *Think of a World without any Flowers*!

Under his own tutelage Colin Morris's BBC blank screen seems to have become more blank! Yet it is people involved in this charade with voices in the religious broadcasting establishment (in the BBC, ITV, and some church advisory bodies) that are the first to criticize the American religious broadcasters we have referred to.

It is all too easy to caricature the American Electronic Church. Some of it, to British eyes and ears, *is* appalling (but many are appalled by some of the BBC and ITV religious programmes). Objections can be raised to the way some of their money is obtained (but many object to the alcohol advertising that is indirectly funding the ITV religious output). However, some of the American material is extremely good. What must not be objected to is the commitment and the

competence of the best of the American religious broadcasters. If you choose the right programmes you are not
bored!

True, some of the American religious broadcasters may
have been seduced by the money. But how many of the
clerics and Christian lay-people in British religious broadcasting have been seduced by the security and the status of
their jobs; and how many give away that proportion of their
salaries that is over and above the national average stipend
for parochial clergy and licensed lay-workers? I expect that
there is a mixed bag here, as there is in America.

12
Free and Fair

One of the main conclusions of the Peacock *Report of the Committee on Financing the BBC* published in July 1986 was as follows:

> The end of all censorship arrangements would be a sign that broadcasting had come to age, like publishing three centuries ago. Prepublication censorship, whether of printed material, plays, films, broadcasting or other creative activities or expressions of opinion, has no place in a free society and we would want to advise Government and Parliament to embark forthwith on a phased programme for ending it.[1]

The Committee reckoned that the public were the best judges of their own interests.

The Committee advocated retaining subsidized Public Service Broadcasting such as the BBC could provide. This would be for programming to promote 'knowledge, culture, criticism and experiment'. But generally what the committee was expecting 'to disappear or much diminish' were 'negative censorious controls. If the right conditions are established, there will be little need for "regulation" apart from the general law of the land to cover matters such as public decency, defamation, sedition, blasphemy and most of the other matters of concern in broadcasting.'[2]

But how can there be such freedom? The reason why this can be proposed as a policy is because the technology is changing very fast. There are now various possibilities through Wideband Cable and Satellites, including Direct Broadcasting by Satellite. No longer can the broadcasting establishment say they are the guardians of a precious commodity—a handful of radio frequencies. Many channels are now possible, and they must be open to access. Also, if we are to see the Christian faith properly in the Public Square and itself accessible, these channels must be *freely* open to the religious community. But there will be opposition.

Already the Peacock Report has been 'rubbished' by various vested interests. We should not be surprised. Broadcasting is in effect a closed shop. Yet is this acceptable and is it not dangerous, as the broadcasters themselves admit, that broadcasting provides them with 'revolutionary' power? That certain people should have a monopoly or duopoly in the control of the spread of ideas is wrong in a democracy. But this happens and it happens nowhere more than in religious broadcasting.

A new deal

Perhaps one of the reasons why the nation has failed to hear the Christian voice in the Public Square as clearly as it should is that the determiners of religious expression in the media have often been liberal modernists. Modernists are people in the church who doubt much of traditional Christianity—the virgin birth of Jesus and his empty tomb, for example. Or even if there is a tentative belief in these doctrines, they think that those orthodox or evangelical Christians who confidently affirm them are probably 'naive' and 'simple believers'. There is thus a possible division of outlook in fundamental matters of belief between broadcasters and the generality of Christians in the nation.

The hey-day of modernism in the Church of England was just when Reith was bowing out as Director-General in 1938.[3] Its effects in terms of influence were strong until the end of the sixties, which was just when Hugh Greene was bowing out. But since then there has been a remarkable resurgence of evangelical (and believing) Christianity in the church at large and especially in the Church of England. Fifty per cent of those being ordained now in the Church of England come from evangelical theological colleges. But because these are younger men, rather than older, the leadership of the Church does not yet represent this strength. Nor, over the years, has this strength been represented in the broadcasting establishment or its output. But it appears that things are changing as evangelicals are being appointed to some positions. But will there be change in output?

As yet the effects of the problem remain. And this problem is that at least some of those involved in the religious broadcasting output must have acted as censors to other Christians and censored out their particular style of faith, their commitment and their proclamation.

Not that it has ever been so crude as the use of a blue pencil. For this censorship operates through the process of programme initiation (these ideas adopted, those ideas excluded or censored); and the process of invitation (these people selected to participate, those people not selected, or more likely, never even thought about).

There is nothing odd about this. To a degree it has to happen. None of us can completely leave our convictions behind. A prime example from 'general' television was Hugh Greene and his decision to censor Mrs Whitehouse, when she was protesting against too much sex and violence on television in the sixties. Greene had a strong conviction 'that Mrs Whitehouse was the sort of person who would have been at home in Nazi Germany or at home in Communist Russia. And that is the sort of thing which through all my early experience I have learnt to hate.' So he vetoed 'the suggestion of a programme about her on the grounds that she thrived on such publicity'.[4] The irony (and the arrogance) was that Greene was accusing Mrs Whitehouse of being the censor!

We shouldn't be surprised if this sort of thing happens in religious television. For that reason the only safe, just and fair course of action is to have 'uncensored' television, including uncensored religious television. This is precisely what the religious broadcasting establishment doesn't want. But the Christian public does want it.

And the focus of fear for the religious broadcasting establishment and, perhaps, other establishments, is American religious television. Indeed, it was the General Synod's Church Information Committee (with BBC and IBA connections and so linked with the broadcasting establishment) that spoke to the Hunt Committee on Cable Television about the Electronic Church and said:

> The very phrase has become synonymous with a debasement of religious programmes on television. The advent of Cable and Satellite Television here will expose this country to the same pressures. It is most important to realize that religious programmes relayed by television are potentially more emotive and manipulative than any other type of programming.[5]

It was *this* committee that wanted religious groups excluded from participation in Cable operating companies and the opportunity to lease channels! But it was the pot calling the kettle black. For the religious broadcasting establishment can be as 'emotive' and 'manipulative' in its own way. And it is all the more serious because of its ability to be subtle and clever.

For example, on April 22nd, 1983, BBC Radio 4 put out a programme called *Electric Gospel* (possibly trying to influence Parliament over the Cable Bill). But its criticism of American religious broadcasting was biased and unbalanced, without a single voice in defence of it. In itself it was a very well-put-together programme. But it was quietly emotive and manipulative.

The Electronic Church

But the General Synod would not go along with its Church Information Committee. It passed a contrary amendment. It was said, indeed, in the debate that these were unfair and sweeping generalizations about the Americans. From the floor it was made clear that although there was room for criticism, there was also room for praise. I personally intervened to make the following points:

> I do not like all of it [the Electronic Church] any more than I like all of ITV (or BBC for that matter). If the style ever came here I'd like to see it modified and I'm sure it would be. A lot of it is of the Terry Wogan chat variety; there are soap operas (and very good too) and there are some excellent children's cartoons. Yes, there are programmes like YTV's *Stars on Sunday* and a lot of it is as good as *Songs of Praise*. There is first class drama by the Lutherans. I've seen an excellent Roman Catholic programme on a Pentecostal network in Los Angeles! Of course there are regular services and crusades featuring well-known evangelists like Billy Graham. But what is wrong with that?[6]

One of the most powerful speeches came from Philip Lovegrove himself a (dissident) member of the Church Information Committee. He mentioned that technical limitations brought about the Public Service philosophy in the twenties. But what that means today is that 'no one in control of broadcasting is elected, either by market forces or by popular vote. Appointments are made in secret by Ministers according to criteria that no one knows anything about.' Yet patronage in broadcasting is dispensed from the BBC to a tune of £100 million annually on drama! 'We see,' he said, 'what has happened with Channel 4, where there is an illusion of participation. Favoured interest groups are certified as OK by the progressive consensus at the centre and air time is given to certain minorities. Well, you have seen the minorities—I wonder whether you would have chosen them. The appointed elite appoint the people and it is a parody of democracy.'[7]

So the Synod ignored the Church Information Committee and informed the Government it *would* support free access for religious bodies in terms of broadcasting. The Evangelical Alliance then supported the General Synod's resolution with its own submission to the Home Secretary. The considerations that influenced its decision, it said, were these:

> Broadcasting in the United Kingdom is not ideologically neutral. The Hunt Committee had been concerned that monopoly services should be free from any kind of ideological bias (Report—section 25). But the facts as we judge them are these. In the 'Reithian' era the ideological values behind both entertainment and analysis programmes were Christian. Since then, however, the values have changed. They are now secular and humanistic if not materialistic. In such a situation we believe it unjust to exclude Christians *as* Christians from direct access to this future development in television. Market forces, we believe, will mean only responsible groups will get involved and then indeed only on a very limited scale. But to exclude religious bodies from direct access to this electronic communication would be in our contemporary culture as intolerable as it would have been centuries ago if they had been excluded from direct access to the printing press!

The Government modified the legislation accordingly— rightly so, as the Hunt Committee had been given advice that was *not* representative of the views of the Synod or the wider church. It was the advice of the religious broadcasting establishment and it was advice that was the result of a certain paranoia.

For in the United Kingdom there is a paranoia about the American Electronic Church which is quite irrational. More sensibly we should realize that with the new technology, with the national strength of evangelicals, with the Peacock proposals for deregulated broadcasting, American-style religious programming is bound to come to the United Kingdom sooner rather than later. One Anglican bishop 'feels there is no need for undue alarm . . . our best protection is the basic irreligiousness of the British people'.[8] But this is cloud-cuckoo land and not facing reality.

The best Christian response, surely, is for the British churches to be rational and *positively* critical. And to do that they need to establish the facts. And there are three facts that must be noted.

First, the Electronic Church in the United States is *not* taking people out of the churches and *not* draining the churches of cash. Colin Morris attacks the Electronic Church quite strongly for forming 'surrogate congregations'[9] and says that 'the mainline Churches . . . found that there was a seepage of "bodies and bucks" away from the pews and collection plates'.[10] But the evidence is to the contrary. A study was undertaken in 1984 by the University of Pennsylvania's Annenberg School of Communications and Gallup. This showed that 'contrary to understandable fears, Gospel TV does not undercut attendance and contributions at local churches. The competing church factions face a common, all powerful enemy: secularized general TV.'[11]

Variety

Secondly, it is wrong to tar all American television with the same brush. Jerry Falwell is a pillar of the Moral Majority. But Jimmy Swaggart, a swashbuckling, jingoistic, Pentecostal, says: 'Anyone with that attitude is potentially dangerous.' Billy Graham, greatly respected, is seen preaching to thousands in his programmes and is now, it would seem, more in the middle of the American political spectrum. Pat Robertson, sophisticated and Yale educated, majors on news and chat in his Christian Broadcasting Network's *700 Club,* and is undoubtedly right wing in his views (but one of his main staff has had British Labour Party connections).

There are flamboyant personalities and there are the straight men like James Kennedy of Fort Lauderdale. 'He tries to "fill the gap" left by flashier preachers, offering formal worship and cerebral sermons.'[12] It is not true to say they are all of a type.

Thirdly, there is competence in American religious broadcasting. For example, in television terms CBN's news is good. This is what you would expect, as most of the staff at CBN have come from secular stations and have fully professional standards. So at a recent conference one of the News Directors said he would resign immediately if his journalistic integrity was threatened by Robertson's own political views.

And the proof of the pudding is in the eating. The *700 Club* reaches 27 million viewers. Nor are these people being duped. 'Everybody thinks the TV preacher is doing a number on people,' says Ben Armstrong, the man who coined the phrase 'Electronic Church', 'but it's the viewer with his hand on the dial who controls the system.'

But that will still not do, one suspects, for Colin Morris. His line of argument in the *Electric Church* programme was to the effect that the gospel is about powerlessness and failure—witness the cross of Christ. Television, especially American television, is all about success and getting audiences. This is therefore a denial of the gospel.

But the conclusion that is then left to be drawn is this: unsuccessful television that doesn't attract large audiences is more Christian! Is this special pleading to justify any weak performance on the part of British religious television? Of course, the gospel centres on the cross, but the cross leads to the resurrection and the power of the Holy Spirit at Pentecost.

A restrained but fair analysis of the American religious scene comes from Myrna Grant, who is an assistant Professor in broadcasting writing at Wheaton Graduate School, Illinois. She says this:

> One of the constructive, commendable things about Christian broadcasting in America is that we haven't lost the field by default. Evangelicals and Christians of many different denominations have understood the importance of media and the potential of media both for teaching and even for evangelizing. Many mistakes have been made, but at least they were on the battlefield.
>
> They have blazed a trail in that way and left mistakes in their wake, so the rest of the world can look and say, 'Here are the excesses, here are the mistakes,' and learn from them . . .
>
> I think the Church on earth today, in a humble way, has got a debt of gratitude that could be paid to America. There is a great deal of criticism, not only in Britain, but in many different other countries, from people who are looking at American Christian programming as possible models for their own countries.
>
> I would like to repeat a quote that D. L. Moody loved to use as he travelled around on his evangelistic campaigns. Very often Moody was criticized for errors he was making in his grammar or his style of preaching. The American evangelist would listen to the criticism and then reply, 'I like my way of doing things rather than your way of not doing them!'[13]

If British Christians could co-operate with the Americans, it might ensure that when 'the Vikings come' (to use Peter Elvy's unfriendly phrase)—and come they will—their offerings or suggestions are devoid of any excesses and are more 'culturally appropriate'.

Necessary checks

The probability, therefore, is that there will be a move nationally in the direction of the Peacock Report. That will lead to greater opportunities in broadcasting for all. But that means opportunity for the bad as well as the good. And obviously it would be a sad thing for the bad to drive out all that is good in British broadcasting as a whole. And there is much that we can justly be proud of in our broadcasting system.

In technical ways and in terms of production we often have the best in the world. Potentially and actually there is much that is good and worth preserving in our establishment religious broadcasting. But the future in Britain, sooner perhaps than we think, is likely to be 'pluriform'. This seems to be the thrust of the Peacock Report. There will be independent, unregulated broadcasting alongside regulated Public Service Broadcasting. And it is proposed that the Public Service Broadcasting should still include religious broadcasting. This would be important for ensuring that nothing in the religious broadcasting area would go by default; and it would ensure in this sector a religious component.

And, of course, all this *has* to happen. It is virtually required by the European Convention on Human Rights. While this recognizes that states can require licenses for broadcasting, these clearly may not be withheld in contravention of the spirit of the convention. This convention and the ruling on licenses was drawn up in 1950 in the days of limited frequencies and long before the modern developments in telecommunication technology. Thus Articles 9 (2) and 10 (1) are relevant:

> 9 (2) Freedom to manifest one's religion or beliefs shall be subject only to such limitations as are prescribed by law and are necessary in a democratic society in the interests of public safety, for the protection of public order, health or morals, or

for the protection of the rights and freedoms of others.

10 (1) Everyone has the right to freedom of expression. This right shall include freedom to hold opinions and to receive and impart information and ideas without interference by public authority and regardless of frontiers. This Article shall not prevent States from requiring the licensing of broadcasting, television or cinema enterprises.

What, however, is to be said about an increase in violent or sexually explicit material that may be allowed in via de-regulated broadcasting? This is something that must be attended to. The Peacock Committee were of the view that the law of the land should be enough. That seems reasonable; but currently the obscenity laws are not very effective. And they do not cover broadcasting except for cable programmes. This is a complex area, but one that must obviously be tidied up and sorted out if there are major new developments in broadcasting.

The existing problem was recognized by Mr Winston Churchill, the Conservative MP and grandson of Sir Winston. During April 1986 (yet another event in that month!) he was attempting to bring television within the scope of the Obscene Publications Act 1959.

Broadcasting and the law

But his Obscene Publication (Protection of Children, etc) (Amendment) Bill was effectively killed in the Commons due to lack of time and because not enough MPs supported the Bill's sponsor. At the critical division there were seventy-nine in favour and eleven against. But such are the rules that he needed 100 in favour to secure the amendments. The Bill may not have got things quite right; or it may simply have been that sympathizers were exhausted with all the other political issues going on that April. Perhaps that is why no political steam could be generated. But the Bill drew attention to a problem. As Lord Goodman said—and he is not in favour of using the law to curb creative talent—we need to ensure 'that the people in charge of programmes at the production end are people of commonsense and social responsibility. Unfortunately, from the evidence of my own eyes, there is some reason to believe that not everyone so employed enjoys these qualifications.'[14]

Mr Churchill informed the Commons that he had received letters in the proportion of nine to one in favour of his Bill. He said that people would be angry if their wishes were frustrated. Everyone but the most myopic viewers knew the broadcasting authorities had failed in their duty. Mr Churchill commented:

> It had been said that last year no fewer than 62 X-rated films were put out by the BBC alone. Millions of parents with small and teenage children were questioning whether the broadcasting authorities had the right, in defiance of their statutory obligation, to put out material which would be held to deprave and corrupt young people.[15]

The Bill caused a stir. In fact it caused a fit of hysteria among the 'creative community'. This was particularly so when they saw Mrs Thatcher go through into the Aye lobby on the second reading. Michael Grade, Controller of BBC 1, headed a group on behalf of the British Academy of Film and Television Arts (BAFTA) to oppose the legislation. With the hyperbole common to these occasions, he said that if the Bill was passed it would mean 'art galleries and museums would need "adults only" rooms for pictures of the crucifixion, Leda and the Swan and Grecian urns!'[16] His own conclusion was: 'Let us stamp out pornography by all means, but let's not throw out the thriving cultural baby with Mrs Whitehouse's dirty bathwater.'[17]

Whatever the precise details concerning this debate, it is now past history. But the problem remains. Michael Grade admits it—'let us stamp out pornography'. It is unfortunate that those nursing the cultural baby tend to identify Mrs Whitehouse as the sole source of opposition to gratuitous sex and violence on television. Again, this shows how the leadership in the media is out of touch with public opinion. There are many who will not agree with Mrs Whitehouse on a number of things but are now saying, 'Enough is enough.'

But to approach the problem of obscenity on television we must look at the issue in a wider context.

13
Cleaning Up

1983 was a year when a number of issues relating to broadcasting came to the surface. This was because of the discussion on Cable Television and Direct Broadcasting by Satellite. It resulted in a new Cable and Broadcasting Act 1984.

But at the end of the year in the House of Lords it became clear that there was considerable worry about the present state of broadcasting. The occasion was the debate on the BBC annual report. Lord Nugent opened the debate by saying that the Government had a compelling obligation to reform and strengthen the obscene publications legislation as a first step to the BBC and IBA restraining offensive material in their television programmes.

He gave examples of what he objected to. First there was a BBC programme for young people. In it they were shown three possible relationships for their future lives. The first was a couple engaged to be conventionally married; the second, a couple not married but 'shacked up' (as it was described); and the third, a couple of homosexuals. 'To teach youngsters,' he said, 'that promiscuity and perverted relationships are a serious alternative to marriage as a way of life is both dangerous and irresponsible. It is treating them as bodies without souls.' But the BBC had apparently defended this as being an educational programme!

His second example was from ITV and showed a picture of the crucifixion with Christ having a cigar in his mouth as an advertisement for cigars. The IBA on this occasion apologized when there were complaints.

Then Lady Lane-Fox said in the debate that a lot of the blame lay with scriptwriters. She had at one time thought of making a career of scriptwriting but found the use of four letter words was advised to make scripts more natural. The Earl of Halsbury, a former governor of the BBC, said that what was lacking was leadership at the top. The type of complaints which Mrs Whitehouse sent to the BBC would have been unthinkable in Lord Reith's day. 'Carlton Greene,' he said, 'who initiated the permissive age liked bawdy jokes, made no secret of it, and did not see what was wrong with it.'[1]

At some point something must be done. But the trouble is that the law as it stands, the Obscene Publications Act 1959, would be ineffective even if it were to cover broadcasting. That is why in 1977 the then Home Secretary appointed a committee under Professor Williams 'to review the laws concerning Obscenity, Indecency and Violence in publications, displays and entertainments'. Actually broadcasting was excluded. But film censorship was to be reviewed. The Committee was then to make recommendations. The Committee reported unanimously in December 1979 in 166 pages, plus eight appendices.

The problem

The Williams Committee expressed the situation that was causing worry like this:

We saw how certain magazines had in recent years been extending the range of what they considered they could show (1.5).
We feel it necessary to say to many people who express liberal sentiments about the principle of adult freedom to choose that we were totally unprepared for the sadistic material that some film makers are prepared to produce . . . Films that exploit a taste for torture and sadistic violence do raise further and disturbing questions (12.8).

But things were made worse because the law had been (and still is) unenforceable. This has in turn affected standards. And the law has been unenforceable because of the words 'deprave and corrupt' in the Obscene Publications Act 1959 and the Theatres Act 1968. This has prevented people from saying that anything is harmful! How do you measure whether you are depraving or corrupting someone sufficiently for a jury to convict?

So because the Obscene Publications Act has not been a tight enough net, those wanting to make money out of pornography have kept up with (or down with) what the law actually allows. But, of course, the intention of those who promoted the 1959 Act was *not* to allow pornography but to allow, as A. P. Herbert said, 'reasonable liberty for honest writers'.[2] However, as the Williams Committee admitted, 'for many years the obscenity laws have been in retreat' (4.2). And the practical result has been a change in standards.

Definitions

So since the 1959 Act the definition of 'obscene' has not been in terms of the object itself, judged in terms of its intrinsic nature. It has been defined in terms of what a magazine or film does to the reader or viewer. So the question is, 'Has it a tendency to deprave and corrupt?' But, as we have said, proof that a given work *as a matter of fact* depraves and corrupts is hard to come by.

For this reason the Board for Social Responsibility of the Church of England's General Synod wanted a more objective and less functional definition of pornography. In its submission to the Williams Committee it said: 'Obscenity exists as an objective reality and a problem independently of the law's attempts to check it.'

By contrast to the Obscene Publications Act, the success of the Customs Act, the Post Office Act and Acts relating to public displays supports this view of the Board for Social Responsibility. These use the test of 'indecent or obscene'. The Williams Committee admitted that tests of indecency were interpreted 'in terms of offence against recognized standards of propriety, and in those proceedings that have been brought, it seems to have given rise to very little practical difficulty' (2.27). A. P. Herbert said, '"Indecency" is comparatively clear and is seldom likely to baffle a jury for long.'

So any new Act or amendment to the present Act probably should include the word 'indecent'. For it is particularly appropriate, as it underlines one of the essential features of all pornography; and that is the crossing of the line between the private and the public. The Williams Committee expressed it like this:

> Pornography essentially involves making public in words, pictures or actual performance the fulfilment of fantasy images of sex or violence. In some cases the images are of forbidden acts; so it is with images of violence. In other cases, the line that is transgressed is only that between private and public; the acts represented in the images would be all right in private but the same acts would be objectionable in public . . . People have strong sentiments attached to these notions of public and private, of what is 'unsuitable'—in its original sense, 'indecent' —to show (7.4).

But if the phrase 'deprave and corrupt' is inadequate, we need also to be careful about the phrase 'offensive to reasonable people'. This was the Committee's choice. But will it be able to exclude the material that should be excluded?

The problem here is this: there is a radical difference between what is 'offensive' in terms of current standards, and what is 'offensive to reasonable people'. The two are not the same. A reasonable person might admit that a certain item offended against standards that they endorsed; but they need not necessarily be *personally* offended by it. Is it always 'offensive to reasonable people' to have nude women in seductive poses on the covers of magazines in the local newsagents? It could be argued that it is 'corrupting of public morals' (to use the Common Law phrase). It could be argued it flouts public decency. But 'offensive' is the wrong word, because it belongs to a wrong category of associations and is not sufficiently objective. It would only rule out the most extreme forms of pornography. But the Director of Public Prosecutions recognizes three grades of pornography, according to the Committee (4.6). All of these need to be considered from the perspective of the general public and certainly in terms of broadcasting.

Objection to pornography has all too often been associated with 'offensiveness' or 'disgust'. This immediately puts it alongside prim and proper 'Victorianism' and smelling salts! But it has to be emphatically asserted that many healthy and reasonable people are not disgusted by much of what is, in reality, pornographic. They judge it nevertheless to be harmful, damaging and indecent. To define pornography exclusively in terms of disgust is to beg a number of questions; and it is to define it only in terms of the most degrading form of pornography.

Of course, at the end of the day there always will be some ambiguity over definition. But that shouldn't mean we don't take action to amend the law. Someone has said, 'If out of a sample of a thousand works of fiction some thirty were branded as obscene but agreement could not be reached . . .

on three others, it would not matter much.'

Harm

In the Williams Report the discussion of the harm that pornography does seemed somewhat confused. Their difficulty
started from their requirement 'that the causation of the
harm should lie "beyond reasonable doubt"' (5.31). Put that
together with some words they quote of Stephen Brody and
you have a recipe for inaction:

> Social research has not been able unambiguously to offer any
> firm assurance that mass media in general and films and tele-
> vision in particular, either exercise a socially harmful effect, *or
> that they do not* (1.9).

But note, first, that Brody was talking about 'mass media
in general' not about pornography! Secondly, he admitted
that while he did not believe television and films mould behaviour, he nevertheless admitted that 'it is in the amplifica-
tion of existing [potentially violent or antisocial] tendencies
that the main influence is likely to lie' (6.18). But if that is
not 'harm', what is?

Thirdly, it is unreasonable to require a causal connection
'beyond reasonable doubt' before wanting to use the law. Of
course it is essential that *once* a law is on the statute book a
person is convicted only when it is beyond reasonable doubt
that he or she has broken the law. This is the principle that
gives security within the law and basic justice.

But the principle of 'beyond reasonable doubt' is by no
means always appropriate in the *drafting* of laws. Take, for
example, the fixing of speed limits on motorways. It is simply
not beyond reasonable doubt that 70 mph is the best limit.
The Americans doubt it and say 50 mph is the best; the
British motoring organizations doubt it and are arguing for
80 mph. There clearly is doubt; but a law *has* to be estab-

lished. If we waited until we were absolutely certain about motorway limits before doing anything, we would have speed merchants in Porsches driving at 150 mph down the M1!

Life cannot wait for absolute certainty. When a decision has to be taken, to fail to act on the ground that there is no absolute proof that a decision is right is, surely, irresponsible. Indeed, in something like pornography, where there is a common presumption that it is harmful, it has to be proved beyond reasonable doubt that it is *harmless*. This is what we do with new drugs on the market. They have to prove their safety. So it should be with pornography.

Fourthly, the arguing of the Committee in 1979 looks tragic now in the late eighties. They argued that in the years preceding their report—when pornography was becoming heavily available—'the increase in sexual offences generally and in rape and sexual assaults, has been significantly slower (though in the case of rape alone the difference is less significant)'. They then referred to 'the contrast between the upward trend in crime generally and the greater stability in the numbers of rapes and sex assaults' (6.41).

Today's facts

But the dam has burst in the eighties. In 1985 sex offences rose by 17%. The number of reported rapes that year rose by 409 to 1,842. And in London it is reckoned that fewer than a third of rape cases are reported. Commenting on the 1985 figures, a worker at the Birmingham Rape Crisis Centre said, 'Dirty magazines and romantic novels were partly to blame for the rising sex crime rate. They all emphasize women being "taken" by smouldering brutes, which contrasts starkly with the reality of rape.'[3]

Of course, there are other reasons for rape. But the American Attorney General, Edwin Meese, had a report from his Commission on Pornography in 1986 which agreed that there is a causal link between violent pornography and aggressive behaviour towards women. Furthermore it said that exposure to sexually explicit material that is not violent but nevertheless degrades women—a category that 'constitutes somewhere between the predominant and the overwhelming portion of what is currently standard fare heterosexual pornography . . . [bears] some causal relationship to the level of sexual violence'.[4] This completely overturned the findings of a 1970 President's Commission on Obscenity and Pornography, which the new report claims is 'starkly obsolete'. In the UK, the Williams Committee Report of 1979 bears the marks of the same obsolescence. Something more positive is needed now.

But there are more subtle forms of harm that come from pornography. Let me mention six. First, there is the harm to literature. Irving Kristol wrote as long ago as 1971 of how much literature was losing from the fact that practically anything could be published now in America. He said that in a free market

> Gresham's Law can work for books or theatre as efficiently as it does for coinage—driving out the good, establishing the debased. The cultural market in the U.S. today is being preempted by dirty books, dirty movies, dirty theatre. A pornographic novel has a far better chance of being published today than a non-pornographic one, and quite a few pretty good novels are not being published at all simply because they are not pornographic, and are therefore less likely to sell. Our cultural condition has not improved as a result of the new freedom.[5]

Secondly, there is the harm to sexual experience itself. When sex is divorced from love, as in pornography, it can lead to a process of sexual desensitization. One actor in a nude play said, 'Initially, perhaps, it is erotic . . . after you've been really saturated . . . [you become] impotent for a while and that is nothing unusual.' The fact that so many refer to the experience of pornography as 'boring' can relate to the same phenomenon. Initially it is sexually arousing, but then it becomes tedious.

Further harms

Thirdly, there is the harm to the creators of pornography—the actors and the models. Jill Tweedie wrote about *Oh Calcutta!*, Kenneth Tynan's pornographic musical review, in the *Guardian*.[6] She protested at the exploitation of actors and actresses who were forced by unemployment to expose themselves in such shows. She speculated about why the show had caused so much absenteeism among the cast. In the Williams Committee Report it was said that 'one of our psychiatric witnesses, Dr Gallwey, suggested to us that there was much misery in the trade and that many of the girls in strip clubs, for example, were disturbed and mentally ill' (6.71).

Fourthly, there is the harm of a more general sort that relates to society. It is hard to measure precisely how society is being affected at a psychological level. But it is not at all unreasonable to suggest that a sex or pornographic culture is going to demotivate communal effort. Viewing a society made up of people who seem happy to tolerate such a culture, an individual may well ask himself, says E. J. Mishan,

> are these the sort of people for whose society he must stand ready to make sacrifices? . . . Can anyone *care* very much what happens to a society whose members are continually and visibly obsessed with sexual carousal—to a society where, in effect, the human animal has been reduced to a life-style that consists in the main activity of alternatively inflaming itself and relieving itself?[7]

Fifthly, there is the harm that pornography does to marriage and the family. It certainly can be argued that anything that reinforces values that condone pre-marital or extramarital sexual activity is harmful to the sanctity of marriage.

And sixthly, it harms women at a fundamental level. By its very nature pornography tends to degrade women and treat them as sexual playthings for men. As Susan Brownmiller says, 'Pornography is virulent propaganda against women. It promotes a climate in which the ideology of rape is not only tolerated but encouraged.'[8]

But it will be objected by those who want little to be done about pornography that it is a symptom of deeper ills in society. It is not the real, underlying cause of harm.

Now that may indeed be true sometimes. But such a sign of underlying ills can itself be a 'cause'. Take someone who is physically ill and has a very high temperature. This fever is a symptom of an underlying infection. Yet the fever can properly be said to be causing a harmful delerious condition. It is sensible to lower the temperature with aspirins or tepid sponging, thus preventing any serious secondary effects from the high temperature. It also encourages the well-being of the patient. It is a tenet of good doctoring that treatment of symptoms is worthwhile even when curative medicine is not available. Symptoms need to be treated while attempts are being made to deal with the underlying cause.

So to conclude: the axiom of the Williams Committee was that 'no conduct should be suppressed by Law unless it can be shown to harm someone' (5.1). Pornography can be shown to be harmful. It should be suppressed by law.

The law

Now, of course, it is right that we should preserve free expression at all costs. This is one of the great achievements of Western liberal democracy; and we must cherish it. But the expression that needs to be free is that of religious, political, ethical and radical *views*—not the expression of obscenities. As we have seen, the freedom to articulate views, however radical (provided the language is not obscene) has existed for centuries in Britain. And up to the sixties it had existed happily alongside the legal *suppression* of the pornographic and obscene.

But we must here distinguish the form of an expression and its content. Take the Committee's statement that they did not believe pornography could be opposed for 'encouraging a view of sex as trivial amusement' (7.18). This was argued for on the grounds that there must be freedom for people to advocate what opinions they want, including a trivial view of sex.

But this seems to be imprecise. For pornography does not *advocate opinions* about sex being trivial, rather it *actually trivializes* sex. It does not argue for a position; it *does* something. It is performative.

There is a world of difference between a book advocating that it ought to be right to publish pornographic photos, and actually publishing pornographic photos. The law should not forbid the expression of this opinion about the right to publish these photos; it is entirely within its rights to forbid such photos being published until that expression of opinion has been generally found convincing, and then democratically voted as a right by law. To date, that and similar opinions in Britain have not been found generally convincing. The law, therefore, should suppress such pornographic productions and publications. As Martin Luther King said, the law cannot change the heart but it can restrain the heartless.[9]

The seriousness of what has been called 'moral pollution' was identified by Paul at the end of the first chapter of Romans. He there draws attention to the sexual practices and temptations of his day. Professor Blaiklock in his commentary on this passage says this:

> The close of this chapter is a warning to all peoples and all ages. To read it in our own 'permissive society' is to encounter a challenge to be strong in faith, determined in our committal to

God, urgent in our evangelism. Paul is describing a society which had abandoned God. He is diagnosing the malady from which Rome was to die, for no great nation has ever been destroyed by a foe from without which has not already destroyed itself by corruption within. Such sin carries its own penalty, its own damnation. The time is here when Christians must show as they were called upon to do in Rome, by word, act and manner of life, their difference.[10]

14
Left, Right and Forward

The church as such must not be allied with any one political party. This is simply because the kingdom of God can never be co-terminous with any one political programme. It is bigger than the confines of a party manifesto. However in the West both the right and the left can often have Christian endorsement.

Left and right

We have seen that two of the great ends of any social order are freedom and fellowship. It can be reasonably argued that the right majors on freedom, while the left on fellowship; the right seeks to restore the balance when the collective state ignores or frustrates personal opportunity and initiative; the left seeks to prevent personal freedoms unfairly frustrating the collective good.

Then again the right is concerned to fulfil the biblical mandate of 'being fruitful and replenishing the earth', for it is concerned with wealth creation. The left, however, is concerned to obey the biblical command to secure justice for the poor and the oppressed; it is concerned with the fair distribution of the wealth that has been created. The dangers respectively are that the right, in its proper concern for wealth creation, ignores certain injustices; on the other hand the left, in its proper concern for justice and distribution, can forget wealth creation, so that before long there is general 'want'!

And the reason why members of the Christian church can find themselves arranged on either side of the right-left divide is this: one person sees a solution proposed by the right as an answer to one problem; another person sees the opposite solution proposed by the left as an answer to *an altogether different problem*. Nuclear power is a classic example. The right sees the development of nuclear power (with all the benefits of a cheaper energy resource) as the long-term answer to a number of economic problems. And a failure to solve these economic problems will cause hardship and frustrate some of the welfare goals society undoubtedly has. But the left sees nuclear power in terms of environmental pollution, competition with mining, health risks, linkage with nuclear weapons and the possibility of a major disaster. To oppose nuclear power solves one set of problems. To support nuclear power solves another. Thus it is foolish nonsense for churchmen to argue that the gospel of Jesus Christ gives you a clear line on which of these approaches is right. It is a balancing of arguments. A decision has to be made in a grey area. So much in politics, contrary to what the parties say, is of this order.

Decisions

But the Christian tradition believes that even in politics you can do more than merely balance arguments. For there is such a thing as divine guidance; and that is not improper in the political sphere any more than in the personal sphere.

In the personal sphere a man or woman may seek guidance about marriage, work, housing, or money. If they are committed Christians they will probably do these three things: think, seek advice *and* pray. They will pray that God guides them. And Christian experience is that he usually does! This is not necessarily in a miraculous way (although sometimes that may be the case), but God guides through circumstances, new evidence coming at the key moment and through a growing consciousness of the right course of action; or, if others are involved, through a growing consensus. James writes in the Bible: 'If any of you lacks wisdom [practical wisdom], let him ask God, who gives to all men generously and without reproaching, and it will be given him' (Jas 1:5).

This was the way great statesmen like Lord Shaftesbury operated. At the height of the Crimean War Lord Palmerston wanted Shaftesbury in his cabinet, and so did the newspapers and the Queen; and his wife was 'pushing'.

> I was at my wit's end [wrote Shaftesbury many years afterwards]. On one side was ranged my wife, relations, friends, ambition, influence; on the other, my own objections, which seemed sometimes to weigh as nothing in comparison with the arguments brought against them. I could not satisfy myself that to accept office was a divine call; I *was* satisfied that God had called me to labour among the poor.

He tried to refuse; but then came a note from Lady Palmerston telling him to put on uniform and be at Buckingham Palace that afternoon to be sworn in! Palmerston was trying to force the issue, as he couldn't find a substitute. Here, however, is Shaftesbury's own record of what happened:

> I seemed to be hurried along without any will of my own; without any power of resistance. I went and dressed, and then, while I was waiting for the carriage I went down on my knees and prayed for counsel, wisdom and understanding. Then, there was

someone at the door; as I thought, to say that the carriage was ready. Instead of that a note, hurriedly written in pencil, was put in my hands. It was from Palmerston. 'Don't go to the Palace.'

'Shaftesbury, middle-aged as he was,' says the biographer John Pollock, 'danced round the room for joy.'[1] Lord Harrowby was willing to fill the post instead.

Why shouldn't politicians operate like this today? Some indeed do. A number of politicians pray together informally. But far more should! After all, life at the 'centre' is not totally different to life at the 'edges'. Economics and budgets at the Exchequer, as we have been told, are not totally different to family housekeeping budgets—you can't spend what you haven't got! Central budgets just add on the noughts! If an unemployed man prays about work opportunities, why shouldn't Government ministers pray for a resolution of the desperate problem of unemployment? There is no easy answer to it, and there is nothing worse than false hopes. But what can be said is this: a change in the moral and religious climate of the nation is an essential element in any solution. And that means that people, somewhere, sometime, will need to start praying for God's help and strength.

At present Parliament starts its day with prayers. How many of the MPs actually *pray* the prayers? Why should this part of Parliamentary procedures not be upgraded? We have upgraded the debates, through television and radio documentaries, news bulletins, and analysis programmes. Perhaps the church needs to upgrade prayer for the nation!

Most of us are too pompous about politics. John Macmurray's description of the state is relevant:

If we track the State to its lair, what shall we find? Merely a collection of overworked and worried gentlemen, not at all unlike ourselves, doing their best to keep the machinery of government working as well as may be, and hard put to it to keep up appearances.[2]

Politicians are just ordinary men and women. They need praying for and they need to pray themselves. And they need to pray not just for personal problems, but for the political problems that affect us all.

Currently, however, some will probably think it is naive to suggest that God might have a view of the rightness or wrongness of certain political policies. But many do not!

We need to remember that in the absence of some transcendent point of reference our politics will simply be a matter of the jostling of interest groups. And that, indeed, is the present state of British politics. It is a process by which various groups attempt to get *their* share of the 'welfare cake'. But that is a symptom that something has gone sadly wrong.

Interest groups

The Christian consensus, still alive in the country today, is attracted to the democratic ideal. Of that there can be no doubt. But this is the ideal of each participating in the future of the nation; it is not the ideal of each simply being able to fight for a share.

But the democratic ideal is losing ground. With the absence of the Christian voice in the Public Square, there is a growing loss of religion in the sense of the essential component in public life that binds men and women together into a social whole. And this is serious.

In the past the various interest groups in our society have wanted to have a say in shaping the future of the nation. They have not only wanted to engage in politics to secure physical benefits. They have wanted to affirm their worth and dignity by contributing to the national debate. That indeed was the motive behind the various rights movements this century (notably the early suffragettes and their desire for votes for women). Their concern was for a voice in directing the nation, as a sign of their equality with men; and this was the motive behind the early civil rights movements worldwide. But things have changed.

From being constantly told (misleadingly) that we are a pluralist society, each separate constituency is now motivated in a totally different way. It is not so much the desire to have a say in the direction of a unified national purpose; it is more the concern simply to get a greater slice of the corporate cake. The idea that there might be a common goal for the nation and that to be involved in setting it was a privilege, is no longer plausible. So each one of the interests groups is now concerned mainly with its own goals—whether these be groups of teachers, miners, rich businessmen, pensioners, civil servants, farmers, or whoever.

The irony is that in a politics of competing interest groups all are losers ultimately. None can win against the majorities that form the big battalion. It is a matter of arithmetic. And so politics becomes more and more frustrating to all concerned. Thus the miners' strike of 1984-1985 failed because it was seen as nothing other than a factional claim. However powerful the miners might be compared to other industrial workers, their struggle was not seen as 'everyone's struggle'; so there was little hope of success.

Having ignored God in public life, we have inevitably a politics of might being right. And in that case the majority will always win. But this is not liberal democracy, where the goal has been to protect smaller interests. We have seen how moral (or immoral!) minorities for too long have tyrannized majorities. But that is no excuse now for ignoring minority interests.

Where are we going?

It is a sick society that is a conflicting set of factions. That is very nearly our present situation. But without a sense of common purpose, what else can there be? It is a myth to think that *any* of the present political parties will by themselves radically alter this state of affairs.

The tragedy at present at General Election time is this: the various political parties make promises concerning the future of Britain; but these are in effect promises to rearrange the furniture while the boat is still sinking. Neither the Conservative, Alliance nor Labour Parties can provide what is needed to solve Britain's social problems. Only the church and the gospel of Jesus Christ can do that.

It is folly to think that a change of government will solve our national problems. That is not to say that one government is as good as another. Given their limited function, governments can do well or they can do badly. And it is right that they should be called to account every five years.

But society is more than the sphere of government, as we have seen. Not only is there in society the sphere of politics and economics. There is, and must be, the sphere of the religious and the moral-cultural order. Therefore, to expect the Government to provide other than Caesar's share is both unreasonable and dangerous. It is the church and the committed Christian community that has to present the claims of God to the nation.

There is thus a desperate urgency for the Christian faith to be heard again in the Public Square. Yet it is vital that it is the *essentials* of the Christian faith that are heard in the Public Square. We do not need a Pelagian gospel. True, we must talk about social justice and personal morality, but only *after* we have talked about the love of God in Jesus Christ.

Moves such as altering the structures of society to reflect a better deal for urban priority areas, on the one hand, or more decent moral standards for the good of family life, on the other hand, are vital, necessary, and a priority for the church; but they will not bring lasting change. Jesus Christ said, 'From within, out of the heart of man, come evil

177

thoughts, fornication, theft, murder, adultery, coveting, wickedness, deceit, licentiousness, envy, slander, pride, foolishness. All these evil things come from within, and they defile a man' (Mk 7:21-23). Men and women themselves have to be changed and given new life. The gospel of God's grace in Jesus Christ and the transforming power of the Holy Spirit is what the nation needs. And that will only happen if the church and Christian people talk about God in the Public Square and not just about political or moral issues.

In 1978 a little book was published, *What's wrong with Britain?*[3] It was described as containing the 'frank, forthright and thought-provoking views of fifteen of the world's most distinguished men'. They included people as diverse as Lord Hailsham, J. B. Priestley, Sir Arnold Weinstock, Harold Lever and Sir Keith Joseph. But there was nothing in the book about the spiritual state of the nation; there was no hint that the nation was under God or 'the Orb set under the Cross' or that 'the whole world is subject to the Power and Empire of Christ' (as the Queen was told at her Coronation). The nearest to it was from Lord Hailsham. But this was not 'gospel' (good news). It was a piece of hopeful moralizing:

> The only way out of our present malaise is a more conscious effort on the part of all walks of life to inculcate and practise our traditional values of patriotism and service, regard for others in different walks of life and with values different from our own, respect for lawful authority and the rule of law on the part of the individual, and organizations claiming to represent him, and an increased regard for individual liberty and responsibility on the part of central and local government authorities.[3]

But the trouble with all moralizing is the 'weakness of the will'. Paul sums it up: 'I do not do the good I want, but the evil I do not want is what I do' (Rom 7:19). Paul's argument is that it is only in the power of the Holy Spirit of Christ that we can begin to solve the problem. Moralizing otherwise makes matters worse, for it *de*moralizes people as they discover they cannot live up to the moral standards demanded.

This is the case in the nation. We have had enough advice and analysis from sociologists, politicians, journalists and, yes, churchmen. We know there is a problem with Britain. What is needed now is a new vision of what God can enable the nation to be and the spiritual resources to move towards that vision. A national repentance is needed, such that God is once again acknowledged in public life.

Beginning at the church

But repentance, or 'rethinking', has to begin with the church. In the New Testament Peter says that judgement begins 'with the household of God' (1 Pet 4:17). So individual committed Christians must be the first to repent. Surely this must therefore mean praying for the strength, courage and desire to witness to Christ *outside* the church in whatever part of the 'public realm' they find themselves.

Then, secondly, Christian congregations or local churches need to repent and to be open to the Spirit of God to lead them to growth and greater effectiveness. In each local area the parish church or the chapel should be a public witness with a high profile for the gospel.

Thirdly, national church structures similarly need repentance and renewing. Sadly some of the central bureaucracies of the church seem to have lost their way, as have some of our national church leaders. But things are changing. In the Church of England there is a new confidence growing and the evangelical faith (literally, the gospel faith) is being heard once again in many places.

Already there are those who are praying and planning to see *a three- or four-fold numerical increase in active church membership by the end of the century*. That can only be good. For even with the church as it is, as John Hapgood says,

'Religious bodies are the largest voluntary agencies in the country, and therefore on any reckoning make a massive contribution to the richness of institutional life, and to the social training and support of individuals.'[4]

But how is the church to witness to the nation itself? Is it meaningful to talk like that anyway? Can the church help the nation as a whole be more aware of God and his claims? I think it can.

First, the church and Christian people need to have a new commitment to the nation. The church needs to promote a new patriotism in Britain. Patriotism is out of fashion, but there can be no national purpose without it. And it is out of fashion because of the loss nationally of an open public acknowledgement of God. For if a nation sees itself under God, it will have no fear of patriotism sliding into totalitarian nationalism. The 'fatherland' can never be absolute, as God alone is absolute. But remove God and the spectre of tyranny or selfish national pride is never far away. But when a nation is under God, loyalty to the nation is always subordinate to loyalty to God. And this will entail a proper respect for other nations.

So if the Christian community itself can rediscover a new national loyalty, it will be able to challenge the nation from strength. In Neuhaus' words, 'Loyalty to a community is the ticket that grants admission to the critical debate about the meaning of that community.' So he makes the important point, 'Effective criticism . . . depends upon rejoining protest to patriotism.'[5]

Secondly, the church and Christian people need to help public debate focus on the spiritual dimension of many of our social and political questions. And that public debate needs to result in some shared values and social goals in Britain as we approach the last decade of the twentieth century. But these depend on fundamental beliefs about society, life and, indeed, death. These are religious questions. We cannot avoid talking about God.

So Christian people need to share and try to commend their own spiritual vision in this attempt to establish social goals. And these goals matter, even if they are never fully attainable. It was R. H. Tawney who said:

> What matters to the health of society is the objective towards which its face is set, and to suggest that it is immaterial in which direction it moves, because, whatever the direction, the goal must always elude it, is not scientific but irrational. It is like using the impossibility of absolute cleanliness as a pretext for rolling in a manure heap, or denying the importance of honesty because no one can be wholly honest.[6]

Finally, in sharing its vision and establishing these goals, the church must remind itself, as well as the nation, of these words—they were first articulated centuries ago in the Old Testament:

> Take heed lest you forget the Lord your God . . . lest, when you have eaten and are full, and have built goodly houses and live in them . . . and your silver and gold is multiplied . . . then your heart be lifted up, and you forget the Lord your God . . . Beware lest you say in your heart, 'My power and the might of my hand have gotten me this wealth.' You shall remember the Lord your God, for it is he who gives you power to get wealth; that he may confirm his covenant which he swore to your fathers . . . And if you forget the Lord your God and go after other gods and serve them and worship them, I solemnly warn you this day that you shall surely perish (Deut 8:11-14, 17-19).

But along with that warning there needs to go the Old Testament promise: 'If my people who are called by my name humble themselves, and pray and seek my face, and turn from their wicked ways, then I will hear from heaven, and will forgive their sin and heal their land' (2 Chron 7:14).

As the psalmist says: 'Blessed is the nation whose God is the Lord' (Ps 33:12).

Notes

Chapter 1: April Fools

1. *The Times,* April 15th 1986.
2. *Time* Magazine, May 12th 1986, p.7.
3. *The Times,* April 30th 1986.
4. General Synod Papers, GS Misc 241, General Synod Office, SW1, April 1986.
5. Quoted by Colin Morris, *God in-a-Box* (Hodder and Stoughton, London, 1984), p. 132.

Chapter 2: The Crisis of Values

1. David Frost, 'Past perfect, present tense', in *The Sunday Times,* August 25th 1985.
2. *The Times,* March 23rd 1966.
3. *The Times,* April 29th 1971.
4. *Third Way*, Vol. 3, No. 6, June 1979, p. 30.
5. *The Times,* May 9th 1986.
6. Gordon Rattray Taylor, *Rethink* (Penguin Books, Middlesex, 1974), p.34.
7. Brian Griffiths, *The Creation of Wealth* (Hodder and Stoughton, London, 1984), p.119.

8. ibid., p.120.
9. Christie Davies, op.cit.
10. Quotations from John Pollock, *Shaftesbury—The Poor Man's Earl* (Hodder and Stoughton, London, 1985).
11. *Church Times,* September 27th 1985.

Chapter 3: Pluralism

1. *Third Way,* Vol.5, No.10, October 1982, p.10ff.
2. See the very important research on the role and influence of the Sunday school in Thomas W. Laqueur, *Religion and Respectability—Sunday Schools and Working Class Culture 1780-1850* (Yale University Press, 1976).
3. Research Report by Jan Harrison, *Attitudes to the Bible, God and the Church* (Bible Society, London, 1983), p.27.
4. Christopher Lamb of the BCMS/CMS *Other Faiths Theological Project* estimates an 'other faiths' figure of 2.7 per cent in *Co-ordinate* No.9, January 1982. But this would probably include some secularized immigrants who would not necessarily now want to be identified as Muslim, Hindu, etc. The UK Christian Handbook 1987/88 Edition, ed. Peter Brierly (MARC Europe, The Evangelical Alliance and the Bible Society, London, 1986) Table 22a, p.148, gives a figure of 2.6 per cent. But 852,000 Muslims are computed by establishing 1) the country of origin of the immigrant population, 2) children born to immigrants within and outside the UK and 3) the proportion of Muslims in the country of origin. The estimate of the Muslim Community from a questionnaire survey would appear to suggest a much smaller figure than 852,000 (*ibid.,* p. 150ff.).
5. Paul Beasley-Murray and Alan Wilkinson, *Turning the Tide* (Bible Society, London, 1981), p.37.
6. C. Peter Wagner, *Stop the World, I want to get on*

(Regal, Glendale, 1974), p.4.

7. From *The Music with the Form and Order of the Service to be performed at the Coronation of Her Most Excellent Majesty Queen Elizabeth II* (Novello, London, 1953), p.14ff.
8. ibid., p.67.

Chapter 4: The Public Square

1. R. J. Neuhaus, *The Naked Public Square* (Eerdmans, Grand Rapids, 1984), p. 146.
2. ibid., p.97.
3. ibid., p.146.
4. ibid., p.147.
5. ibid., p.17ff.
6. John Stott, *Issues facing Christians Today* (Marshalls, Basingstoke, 1984), p.48.
7. ibid., p.50.
8. ibid., p.52.
9. op. cit., p.142.

Chapter 5: Aims and Axioms

1. *The Times,* January 27th 1975.
2. V. A. Demant, *Religion and the Decline of Capitalism* (Faber and Faber Ltd, London, 1952), p.63.
3. John Stuart Mill, *Utilitarianism, Liberty and Representative Government* (J. M. Dent and Sons Ltd, London, 1910), p.68.
4. op. cit., p.64.
5. ibid., p.65.
6. ibid., p.66.
7. ibid., p.67.
8. op. cit., p.21.
9. Quoted in Gordon Ratray Taylor, op. cit., p.33ff.

Chapter 6: The Biblical Tradition

1. From *The Prologue of the Wisdom of Jesus, the Son of Sirach,* the Apocrypha.
2. G. E. Ladd, *The Presence of the Future* (SPCK, London, 1974), p.94.
3. 2 Esdras 4:36-37.
4. op. cit., p.101.
5. William Barclay, *Ethics in a Permissive Society* (Collins, London, 1971), p.173.
6. ibid., p.174.
7. G. B. Caird, *Saint Luke* (Penguin Books, Middlesex, 1963), p.222.

Chapter 7: Secularism and Liberalism

1. Charles Gore, *Christ and Society* (George Allen and Unwin, London, 1928), p.91.
2. Tertullian, *Ad Scapulam* ('nec religionis est cogere religionem').
3. Athanasius, *De Incarnatione,* 52.
4. Gore, op.cit., p.92.
5. Thomas Aquinas, *Summa Theologiae,* II-II. 4 2.
6. Thomas Hobbes, *Leviathan* (J. M. Dent, London, 1914), p.65.
7. Ernst Troeltsh, *The Social Teaching of the Christian Churches* (George Allen and Unwin, London, 1931), Vol.2, p.1010.
8. Christopher Dawson, *The Historic Reality of Christian Culture* (Routledge and Kegan Paul Ltd, London, 1960), p.46.
9. John Stuart Mill, op.cit., p.73.
10. William Temple, *Christianity and the State* (Macmillan, London, 1929), p.80.
11. John Stuart Mill, op.cit., p.79.
12. R. J. Neuhaus, op.cit., p.148.
13. David Lyon, 'Secularization: the fate of faith in

modern society', *Themelios,* Vol. 10, No. 1, September 1984, p.14.

14. ibid., p.15.

Chapter 8: William Temple

1. E. R. Norman, *Church and Society in England 1770-1970* (Clarendon Press, Oxford, 1976), p.281.
2. William Temple, *The Kingdom of God* (Macmillan, London, 1912), p.90.
3. William Temple, *Christianity and the State,* op.cit., p.109.
4. William Temple, *Christianity and the Social Order* (Penguin, Middlesex, 1942), p.27.
5. ibid., p.27.
6. ibid., p.32.
7. ibid., p.50.
8. ibid., p.74.
9. ibid., p.70.
10. ibid., p.71.
11. William Temple, *Christianity and the State,* op.cit., p.83.
12. ibid., p.83.
13. William Temple, *Christianity and the Social Order,* op.cit., p.51.
14. ibid., p.51.
15. ibid., p.50.
16. Charles Elliott, 'Vision and Utopia', *Theology,* vol. LXXXI, May 1978, p.172ff.
17. William Temple, *Christianity and the Social Order.* op.cit., p.52.
18. ibid., pp.52-53.
19. ibid., p.54.
20. ibid., p.54.
21. ibid., p.121.

Chapter 9: Democracy and the Family

1. Jacques Maritain, *Man and the State* (University of Chicago Press, Chicago, 1951), p.111.
2. Research and Forecasts, Inc., New York City, *Report on American Values in the 80s* (Hartford: Connecticut Mutual Life Insurance Company, April 1981).
3. Warren T. Brookes, 'Goodness and the GNP' in *Is Capitalism Christian?*, ed. Franky Schaeffer (Crossway Books, Illinois, 1985), p.22.
4. ibid., p.23.
5. *The Times,* July 21st 1986.
6. In the United States this proportion is 80% (Warren Brookes, op.cit., p.24); Penny Perrick, a British Journalist, quotes a Home Office Research Study in 1985 as denying such a link [in the United Kingdom] (*The Times*, August 4th 1986).
7. Karl Marx and Friedrich Engels, *The Communist Manifesto* (Penguin, Middlesex, 1967), p.101.
8. D. Cooper, *The Grammar of Living* (Penguin, Middlesex, 1974). p.14.
9. Quoted by Joseph Sobran, 'What Is This Thing Called Sex?' *National Review,* December 31st 1980, pp.1604-05.
10. Michael Novak, *The Spirit of Democratic Capitalism* (Touchstone, New York, 1982), p.159.
11. ibid., p.162.
12. ibid., p.163.
13. ibid., p.164.
14. *The Times,* August 1st 1986.
15. *The Times,* June 11th 1986.
16. *The Times,* May 29th 1986.

Chapter 10: A Tale of Two Men

1. Colin Morris, op.cit., p.7.
2. David Winter, 'Trouble in the air?', *Third Way,* Vol.8,

No.11, November 1985, p.7.

3. op.cit., p.117.
4. op.cit., p.87.
5. Quoted by Colin Morris, op.cit., p.92.
6. ibid., p.93.
7. ibid., p.94.
8. In Basil Mitchell, *Broadcasting, Society and the Church* (CIO, London, 1973) quoted by Colin Morris, ibid., p.116.
9. ibid., p.116.
10. Hansard, Vol. 44, No. 11, Thursday June 30th 1983, p.740.
11. 'Greene, Whitehouse, and the BBC', *The Observer*, August 14th 1983.
12. Quoted by Andrew Quicke, *Tomorrow's Television* (Lion, Berkhamstead, 1976), p.173.
13. ibid., p.171.

Chapter 11: Hidden Censors

1. William Temple, *Christianity and the State*, op.cit., p.14.
2. Professor Alan Peacock, *Report of the Committee on Financing the BBC* (HMSO, London, 1986), p.5.
3. *Church of England Newspaper*, August 1st 1986.
4. *Encounter*, May 1970.
5. Malcolm Muggeridge, *Christ and the Media* (Hodder and Stoughton, London, 1977), p.49.
6. ibid., p.39ff.
7. Quoted by Malcolm Muggeridge, ibid., p.67.
8. ibid., p.64.
9. David Winter, op.cit., p.6.
10. Quoted by Rael and Erich Isaac, 'The Media—Shield of the Utopians' in *Is Capitalism Christian?*, op.cit., p.212.
11. ibid., p.227.

12.   *The Observer,* March 5th 1972.
13.   *The Times,* August 22nd 1983.

Chapter 12: Free and Fair

1.   op.cit., section 696, p.150.
2.   ibid., section 549, p.133.
3.   See David Holloway, *The Church of England—where is it going?* (Kingsway, Eastbourne, 1985), p.77ff.
4.   *The Observer,* August 14th 1983.
5.   General Synod Report, *Cable Television* (CIO, London, 1982), p.12.
6.   General Synod February Group of Sessions 1983, *Report of Proceedings* (CIO, London), p.324.
7.   ibid., p.317ff.
8.   Peter Elvy, *Buying Time* (McCrimmons, Essex, 1986), p.149.
9.   BBC Radio 4, *Electric Gospel,* April 22nd 1983.
10.   *God in-a-Box,* op.cit., p.193.
11.   'Power, Glory and Politics', *Time* magazine, February 17th 1986, p.69.
12.   ibid., p.68.
13.   Quoted by Dan Wooding, 'Tune-in-Church', *Buzz,* June 1983.
14.   *The Times,* April 25th 1986.
15.   *The Times,* April 26th 1986.
16.   *The Sunday Times,* February 23rd 1986.
17.   *The Observer,* February 23rd 1986.

Chapter 13: Cleaning Up

1.   *The Times,* December 15th 1983.
2.   *The Times,* August 26th 1970.
3.   *Sunday Mirror,* March 16th 1986.
4.   'Sex Busters', *Time* magazine, July 21st 1986, p.28.
5.   *New York Times* magazine, March 28th 1971.
6.   *The Guardian,* October 11th 1971—see Peter Cousins,

Christianity and Sexual Liberation (Paternoster Press, Exeter, 1972), p.27.
7. E. J. Mishan, *Encounter,* March 1970, p.27.
8. *Time* magazine, July 21st 1986, p.32.
9. Quoted in *The Longford Report* (Coronet, London, 1972), p.84.
10. E. M. Blaiklock, *Understanding the New Testament—Romans* (Scripture Union, London, 1978), p.9ff.

Chapter 14: Left, Right and Forward
1. John Pollock, *Shaftesbury,* op.cit., p.114.
2. Quoted by John Hapgood, *Church and Nation* (Darton, Longman and Todd, London, 1983), p.57.
3. Patrick Hunter (ed.), *What's Wrong with Britain?* (Sphere Books, London, 1978), p.46.
4. John Hapgood, *Church and Nation,* op.cit., p.49.
5. R. J. Neuhaus, *The Naked Public Square,* op.cit., p.73.
6. Quoted by Duncan B. Forrester, *Christianity and the Future of Welfare* (Epworth Press, London, 1985), p.31.

The Church of England
Where Is It Going?

by David Holloway

Your view of the Church of England will depend largely on your own experiences within its fine historical walls. You may know the warmth of Christian fellowship there, or you may think more of cold and decay.

Then there is the media's image. A slightly humorous, largely irrelevant organization, where ornate buildings and unknown bishops conspire to keep Christianity away from the twentieth century in a breathtaking blur of indecision and doctrinal haze.

So when the spotlight fell on the personal views of the Bishop of Durham, the whole Church seemed to be on trial: what *does* it believe about the Virgin Birth of Jesus, and his Empty Tomb?

David Holloway is one of the clergy in the North-East most anxious to clear the mist of uncertainty and debate. Here he provides an in-depth assessment of the doctrinal and practical issues raised by the controversy. The result is a strategy for both clergy and people, to take up their responsibility to God and the nation—before it is too late.

David Holloway is Vicar of Jesmond, Newcastle-upon-Tyne.

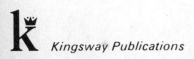

Kingsway Publications

Hope for the Church of England?

Edited by Gavin Reid

Large format paperback

The Church of England has reached a crisis point. Declining numbers, the rise of exciting new alternatives, doctrinal uncertainty, political controversy, and heated debate over the role of women have all served to add to the tensions of a Church that has long sought to be comprehensive in its embrace of opinions and beliefs.

Many are sensing decline. Some have 'abandoned ship', leaving an unease in both the pulpit and the pew.

But is this the whole story?

The men and women who write here are committed first and foremost to Christ. But they all share the belief that the Church of England is still the right way to serve both their Lord and the community around them. They are committed to the Church they love, but they long to see change where it is long overdue. Here we see theological argument and pastoral experience combine to cast more than one ray of hope for the future of a Church which God has been pleased to bless so richly.

The contributors are:
Gavin Reid, John R. W. Stott, Bishop Peter Hall,
Bishop Colin Buchanan, Sir Timothy Hoare, Christopher Idle,
John Richardson, Ian Bunting, Tom Walker, June Osborne,
Julia Wills, Peter Broadbent, George Carey, Ruth Etchells,
Mark Birchall.

k
Kingsway Publications